The Author

James R. Evans: A businessman, an author, a
lecturer and television commentator. Evans
is president of L. G. Evans and Company of
Chicago, a member and trustee of The Philadelphia Society, and chairman of the Illinois
Conservative Union. He has appeared as a
guest commentator on Channel 11 (P.B.S.) in
Chicago.

AMERICA'S CHOICE

Twilight's Last Gleaming
or
Dawn's Early Light

by

James R. Evans

A Fisher Institute Publication

First Printing May, 1981
Second Printing June, 1981

Copyright © 1981 by The Fisher Institute

This edition has been produced as part of the
publishing program of The Fisher Institute.

ISBN: 0-933028-16-4 (paperback)
ISBN: 0-933028-17-2 (hardcover)

Library Of Congress Catalogue Number 80-71089
Printed in the United States of America

ABOUT THE AUTHOR

James R. Evans is a businessman, a student, an author and lecturer.

He is a graduate of the University of Michigan and serves as the president of L. G. Evans and Company, an Illinois firm involved in engineering and machine tool distribution. He is a past president of the American Machine Tool Distributors Association.

He is a veteran of World War II, having served as an officer with the Thirteenth Air Force in the South Pacific theatre.

Over twenty years ago, Mr. Evans embarked upon a course of study involving several hundred volumes covering theology, history, economics, philosophy and political science. A number of these are listed in the general bibliography contained within this volume.

These inquiries culminated in over a hundred lectures and his first book, "The Glorious Quest — Reflections on American Political Philosophy" published in 1967 by Charles Hallberg and Company.

Mr. Evans is a member and trustee of the Philadelphia Society and is chairman of the Illinois Conservative Union, (affiliated with the American Conservative Union of Washington, D.C.) and has appeared as a regular guest commentator on Channel 11, P.B.S. television, Chicago, Illinois.

"He has created a multitude of New Offices, and sent hither swarms of Officers *to harass our people,* and eat out their substance."

Declaration of Independence

July 4, 1776

ACKNOWLEDGEMENTS

I am indebted to innumerable men and women of generations past and present for their enlightenment and encouragement.

There is one man, perhaps more than any other, to whom students of liberty owe a great debt.

He is Leonard E. Read, President of the Foundation for Economic Education (Irvington-on-Hudson, New York) since its beginning in 1946.

A founding member of the Mont Pelerin Society and author of more than twenty-seven books, Leonard E. Read has been an unbending champion of the values underlying individual liberty and a free market so essential to the creation and survival of a free and ordered society.

He, more than anyone, inspired this book.

And a special thanks to Dori Evans, my partner in the exciting exploration of ideas, for her great thoughts and countless hours at the typewriter.

TABLE OF CONTENTS

Part I

Government — The Problem

Part II
The History And The Principles

Part III
The Solutions

FOREWORD

The emphasis, as the Reagan program gets its early formulations, is all on economic principles. That, for the moment, is probably what it should be. If we can't stop inflation from escalating, if we can't lure people into saving a fair proportion of their incomes for capital formation and the correlative creating of new jobs, the State will move in simply because of the demands of frustrated voters. It would be hard then to recover from a crippling socialism.

There are deeper issues, however, than any implied by the concentration on the current fight between "supply-side" and "aggregate-demand" economists. When Congressman Jack Kemp, armed with the Laffer Curve, argues that this proposed across-the-board thirty percent income tax cut will bring incentives to save and to produce back into the economic picture, he is probably right. At least it is worth a try. Of course, the efficacy of the cure depends on the fickle human being. Some politicians have expressed the fear that beneficiaries of Kemp-Roth in the lower tax brackets will prefer to spend their new-found money on McDonald Big Macs while the upper-bracket folk will still go looking for tax-exempt bonds.

Well, what if things don't quite go as Jack Kemp and Arthur Laffer and the other partisans of Reaganomics hope? A deeper issue at stake involves the right of a people to control their own incomes. As Milton Friedman puts it, people have a right to choose. The market should be allowed to correct their mistakes.

The author of *America's Choice: Twilight's Last Gleaming or Dawn's Early Light,* James R. Evans, is a businessman and a war veteran. He is also a patriot who can't bear to see his country torn from its original philosophical moorings. You will find lots of economics, lots of Jack Kemp practicality, in this book. But you will also find a fundamental concern with the nature of man.

Underlying the whole current political fight is the question of where and how we, as a people, derive our rights. If they are the gift of the State, there can be no way in a democracy of keeping fifty-one percent of a pragmatic population from despoiling the minority of 49 percent. That is what the historian Thomas Babington Macaulay feared would happen in America. The other assumption is that rights are somehow ingrained in the nature of the universe that has produced, whether by evolution or divine creation, a human race that is capable of moral insights and an intuitive certainty that there is a God-given order in the cosmos.

Mr. Evans holds that rights are antecedent to political organization. The right to life does not depend on State permission. Once this is settled (as it was by our Founding Fathers), other things follow. To live one must have a right to one's earnings. The compulsory Transfer Society is a philosophical denial of this principle.

Mr. Evans has spent his mature life pondering the literature of freedom. He has had many masters, most of whom he generously quotes. His own contribution is to make principles kinetic. I defy anybody of reasonable intelligence to read Mr. Evans' book without being moved to do something to make the freedom to choose both a personal and a societal reality.

John Chamberlain
Syndicated News Columnist
1981

INTRODUCTION

If, as Noah Webster put it, "God grants liberty only to those who love it and are willing to fight for it!," our United States of America might well be tottering on the brink of a long slide into the abyss of tyranny.

There is overwhelming evidence that American Freedom is declining and soon will be only a memory. Almost no one will state that he is against individual liberty, but a substantial majority of Americans simultaneously propose, support, or at least fail to reject scheme after scheme that limits their liberty, raises their taxes, grants the state powers over their lives, or trades security for government control.

Are our personal freedoms dependent upon our economic freedoms? This volume will contend that they are!

This book was not, at its inception, intended as an exposé, but that is what it became as I began examining the performance of government as it oversees the affairs of citizens. Any search for truth leads where it leads, without prejudice or preconception. This book evolved into an exposure of the consequences of abandoning a value structure for political expediency.

In one sense it is not entirely new. A decade ago this author wrote a small volume entitled *The Glorious Quest — Reflections On American Political Philosophy* (Charles Hallberg & Company, Chicago, Illinois) and some of the thoughts contained therein are part of this volume. Further study, additional analysis, and drastic changes in the state of human liberty within the United States have impelled me to renew my efforts to define the essential ingredients of a free society.

The ideas expressed within these pages are not directed to, nor are they concerned with, liberals, conservatives, Democrats or Republicans. They should concern us **all**!

The ideas expressed are directed to scholars, businessmen, lawyers, doctors, engineers, teachers, students, housewives — in fact, all who are concerned about the darkening relationship between the people of the United States and their government.

One of the major purposes of this book is to describe the incredible growth of government in terms of costs, people, and intervention in our daily lives.

Whether the future of our free republic and its institutions is blessed or doomed (or to what degree of either) will be left to the reader to decide.

It seems, at least to this writer, that most American citizens have accepted the ideas that have permeated American politics for the past four decades without questioning their validity. This book is for them. There are people, of course, who have no identifiable political philosophy, and this book is written for them also. The increasing burden of the state on all of our lives and the lives of our children demands that serious thought be given to the subject. It is more than our responsibility, it is our duty if we expect to participate in the determination of our own futures.

Some of us, regardless of our livelihood, possess deep, heartfelt beliefs and values concerning this Man-Government relationship. Unfortunately, in spite of the strength of our convictions, we often have trouble defending our beliefs and values. This book is written as a clarification and restatement of political principles in hope of overcoming this inadequacy.

As a businessman involved in engineering, I have been aware for years that almost every facet of business, engineering, and science involves measurement in terms of some reliable unit, irrevocable truth, or physical law. Aristotle based his teachings on the fundamental concept that logic is the foundation of philosophy, and in proper logic, the existence and recognition of self-evident first principles or premises was vital. Obviously, any study of the proper relationship between Man and Government would have to begin with a search for these first principles.

There is a tendency on the part of the student to seek out the thinking and writing of those supporting his preconceptions. Any properly directed search for truth must involve, however, an examination of conflicting thought. It is painful at times, and yet fruitful, to examine dissenting opinions.

I hasten to add that regardless of how thorough one's studies, they will not provide either final solutions to our problems or even answers to all the questions. They serve only to open the door to the vastness of ideas.

The time has come to regenerate an interest in **the foundations of a free and ordered society** and thus broaden our understanding of its basic principles and traditions.

My only hope is that upon the turn of the final page the reader will say, "I never thought of it quite that way before, and perhaps I'd better begin to consider political ideas with a little more care."

JAMES R. EVANS

1981

Part I

Government — The Problem

"Government grows like fungus in wet weather."

Maxwell Anderson

CHAPTER I

HOW BIG IS IT?

Thomas Jefferson, in his first inaugural address, defined the aims of his administration as follows:

"A wise and frugal government which shall restrain men from injuring one another, shall leave them otherwise free to regulate their own pursuits of industry and improve them and shall not take from the mouth of labor the bread it has earned. This is the sum of good government."

In general terms, Jefferson's view of the role of government represents the traditional imperatives for individual liberty as viewed by our founding fathers.

How big is government in 1980? Any assessment must be made in terms of some reference and, from an empirical point of view, the casual reference to annual budgets exceeding $500,000,000,000 (five hundred billion dollars) simply buries us in zeros beyond the point of comprehension. For purposes of clarification, let us use an example: If you possessed **one** billion dollars on the day that Christ was born and proceeded to throw it away at a rate of $1,000 every day, today, 1981 years later, you could continue to throw away $1,000 daily for an additional 758 more years before you would be rid of your **one** billion dollars!

Remember that **every dollar spent by government must come from the pockets of you and your fellow citizens in the form of taxes or inflation.**

Another reference should be the moral standard of right and wrong in terms of a proper Man-Government relationship. I should like to quote from an address by Ezra Taft Benson, former Secretary of Agriculture and former President of the Council of Twelve of the Church of Jesus Christ of Latter Day Saints:

A government is nothing more or less than a group of citizens who have been hired by the rest of us to perform certain responsibilities which have been authorized. The government itself has no innate power or privilege to do anything. Its only source of authority and power is from the people who created it.

Keep in mind that the people who have created the government can give to that government only such powers as they themselves have. They cannot give that which they do not possess.

In a primitive state, there is no doubt that each man would be justified in using force, if necessary, to defend himself against physical harm, against theft of the fruits of his labor, and against enslavement by another.

Indeed, the early pioneers found that a great deal of their time and energy was being spent defending themselves, their property, and their liberty. For man to prosper, he cannot afford to spend his time constantly guarding his family, his fields, and his property against attack and theft. When he joins together with his neighbors and hires a sheriff, government is born. The individual citizens delegate to the sheriff their unquestionable right to protect themselves. The sheriff now does for them only that which they had the right to do for themselves — nothing more.

But, suppose pioneer "A" wants another horse for his wagon. He doesn't have the money to buy one, but, since pioneer "B" has an extra horse, he decides he is entitled to share in his neighbor's good fortune. Is he entitled to take his neighbor's horse? Obviously not! If his neighbor wishes to give it or lend it, that is another question. But so long as pioneer "B" wishes to keep his property, pioneer "A" has no just claim to it.

If "A" has no proper power to take "B's" property, can he delegate any such power to the Sheriff? No! Even if everyone in the community desires that "B" give his extra horse to "A", they have no right, individually or collectively to force him to do it.[1] **They cannot delegate a power they themselves do not have. The creation cannot exceed the creator.** With these premises in mind, let us ask the question. **Just how big is government?**

In 1929, Federal expenditures came to 2.6 billion dollars. By 1934, the Federal budget had risen to 6.3 billion; by 1949 to 39.4 billion; by 1956 to 66.2 billion; and by 1960 to 76.5 billion.[2]

In short, it took more than 186 years for the federal budget to reach the 100 billion dollar figure — a line it crossed in 1962.

It required only nine additional years to double the cost of government to over 200 billion dollars per year; only six additional years to double it again to over 400 billion dollars annually, and only three more years to reach 564 billion dollars in 1980. This represents a 21,000 percent increase over the last 50 years, while America's population was growing from approximately 120 million to approximately 220 million — an increase of 83 percent. Federal expenditures have escalated 250 times as fast as the population. (State and local expenditures during the same period have increased approximately 1,000 percent.)[3]

How big is it? In 1929, there were roughly 28 million Americans employed in the private sector and by 1971 this figure had risen to over 57 million. In 1929, there were just over 3 million people on government payrolls and by 1971 there were more than 14 million on the public payrolls. In short, while employment rose 104 percent, government employment rose more than three times as rapidly during that period.[4]

If we include the corresponding increases in the Nation's welfare population, which has grown to approximately 15 million, we are dealing with approximately 30 million people who are directly supported by you, the taxpayer — and this does not include many millions more who are recipients of subsidies, direct or indirect, from various levels of government.

How big is it? Present tax loads on the American worker represent 44 percent of the Nation's personal income. Taxes for the average American outstrip all other costs of living including food, clothing, housing, and transportation! In short, the average citizen must work from January first through May tenth for the government before he even begins to work for himself! To put it another way, the average American citizen works three hours out of every eight hour day just to meet his tax bills.[5]

How big is it? The Federal government owns over 924 million acres of American land — roughly 42% of our total geography.[6]

How big is it? The Federal government spends more than one million dollars of your money every minute of every day.

How big is it? A study by the Ford Motor Company economists shows that there are more people being supported by taxes in the United States (80,655,000) than there are people working in the private sector of the economy to pay the taxes, (71,650,000).[7]

How big is it? Federal paperwork alone costs the American taxpayer almost 40 billion dollars annually! Washington generates enough forms every year to fill 50 major league baseball stadiums![8]

American business spends 130 million man-hours per year filling out those government forms and that cost is passed directly on to the American consumer in the form of increased prices.

How big is it? There are, at the Federal level alone, more than 50 regulatory agencies and bureaus and more than 1,307 Advisory Boards, Committees, etc. — all at the taxpayer's expense.[9]

How big is it? It has been estimated by leading economists that the regulatory agencies (O.S.H.A., E.P.A., C.A.B., F.T.C., et al) added more than 100 billion dollars to consumer prices during the year 1975 alone!

How big is it? In addition to the devastating effect of taxes, government spending beyond its income has created inflation to such an incredible degree that it has devalued our savings by more than 60 percent in the past ten years!

The above figures are indeed staggering and yet they represent but a fraction of the problem.

Unfortunately, these horrendous totals only represent actual expenditures — they do not cover committed future expenditures.

Arthur Andersen & Company, one of the nation's largest C.P.A. firms, has asked the following question: "How can government properly measure the cost, efficiency, productiveity, and impact of its programs and develop costs for the service it provides without using accrual accounting that includes all costs?" The United States government keeps its books on a "cash basis" that simply does not reflect committed financial obligations beyond the current years. Almost all American business corporations, large and small, keep their financial records on an accrual basis because it is the only method that reflects true condition and doesn't hide committed future costs.[10]

According to the National Taxpayers Union, the so-called "debt" represents but a small fraction of the total future financial obligations of the government. Consider these Treasury Department figures as of July 1979.

Public debt:	$ 800,000,000
Accounts payable:	90,000,000
Undelivered orders:	377,000,000
Long term contracts:	19,000,000
Loan & Credit guarantees:	230,000,000
Insurance commitments:	2,078,000,000
Annuity programs:	4,571,000,000
Unadjudicated claims International commitments & Other Financial obligations:	846,000,000[11]

The above figures represent a total financial obligation of $9,011,000,000,000. If you find the "0's" difficult to comprehend, this is more than nine trillion dollars! Do you remember our example of just how much one billion dollars really is? If we convert that to one trillion dollars, it can be said that you could throw away one million dollars every day for 2,739 years before you would run out of money!

To bring these astronomical numbers into something both you and I can understand, consider that every man, woman, and child in the United States has a personal debt of $40,959. and every family of four owes $163,836!

That's how big it is!

"He that is extravagant will soon become poor, and poverty will enforce dependence and invite corruption."

Samuel Johnson

CHAPTER II

WHERE DOES YOUR MONEY GO?

Synergism is best described as a condition in which the results of combining factors tend to exceed the sum total of those factors. It's a good word to describe what has happened in the public sector in recent decades. The impact and growth of government are even greater than the taxes and legislation that created it. In addition, regimentation in the economic sphere breeds inexorable consequences of the same order in the personal realm. As the previous chapter demonstrated, government is, indeed, a classic synergism.

As we examine where your money is going, consider carefully whether or not you would voluntarily spend it on such things if the choice were yours. Reflect, in addition, whether or not such activities should properly be part of government functions, financed from your paycheck.

Before continuing our examination let us, for reemphasis, refer to the ideas of James Madison on this subject as expressed in his *Federalist Paper 45.*

The powers delegated by the proposed Constitution to the Federal Government are few and defined. Those which are to remain to the State governments are numerous and indefinite. The former will be principally on external objects, as war, peace, negotiations, and foreign commerce; with which last power of taxation will, for the most part, be connected. The power reserved to the several States will extend to all the objects which, in the ordinary course of affairs, concern the lives, liberty and properties of the people and the internal order, improvement and prosperity of the State.

Those lamenting the skyrocketing costs of government generally select the Pentagon, Department of Defense, or the "Military - Industrial complex" as the cause.

It simply isn't true!

Does the Department of Defense waste your money? You bet it does. All government activities tend, by their very nature, to be inefficient and wasteful. Is the Department of Defense the primary contributor to massive increases in the cost of government? The truth is that, of all areas of government spending, military expenditures have experienced the slowest growth rate, represented by a constantly diminishing percentage of Federal spending.

During the last 24 years, military spending increased by 113 percent while total Federal expenditures increased by over 463 percent and nondefense spending leaped by over 800 percent.[1]

In 1952, almost 50 percent of the budget was devoted to defense. By 1975 that figure had dropped to 21 percent. For the year 1980, defense expenditures accounted for approximately 23 percent of our total Federal budget.[2]

The above figures are particularly alarming in view of the fact that, since 1960, Soviet military manpower has grown from 3 million to over 4.4 million men under arms. That is more than twice the size of the United States military manpower, which is now roughly one-half million men below the Eisenhower years. In addition, our Navy has dropped from over 900 to fewer than 500 ships while the Soviet Navy has reached what is probably a dominant position. In the area of nuclear missiles, we have gone from an estimated 2 to 1 advantage to a 3 to 1 disadvantage — and the gap appears to be widening.

By any measurement, our military expenditures continue to fall at an alarming rate, while the Soviet strains its economy to achieve military superiority.

If the Department of Defense is not the culprit, then who is the pick-pocket that has been vacuuming your wallet at such an alarming rate? The answer is not difficult. The primary responsibility is readily located in the Great Society programs initiated during the 1960s. Your taxes are paying for education, health care, poverty, food stamps, public housing, model cities, welfare, and similar programs.

The Department of Health Education and Welfare alone represents an increase in spending from 1.0 billion dollars to over 94 billion dollars over the last twenty years — a leap of almost 5,000 percent.[3]

Have these expenditures in the areas of social welfare and education been a sound and successful investment of your earnings? Have they, even to a reasonable extent, benefited those for whom they were allegedly created?

M. Stanton Evans, in his fine expose of the course of American government *(Clear and Present Dangers,* Harcourt, Brace, Jovanovich Inc., 1975), reveals the following anomaly:

> The extent to which social welfare spending is a device for providing government functionaries a living at the expense of everyone else may be gauged by considering the enormous increase in this spending over the decade of the 1960s. As we have seen, social welfare outlays at all levels of government increased by $120 billion between 1960 and 1971 — from $50 billion to $171 billion. This enormous expenditure went into creating poverty bureaucracies, increasing official salaries, building new schools, conducting studies of poverty problems, paying consultants, improving compensation for teachers and administrators, and so on. Some of the spending increase actually reached the poor people in the ghettos, but most of it perforce did not — as may be readily demonstrated.

Poverty estimates in this country vary widely, but the census figures tell us there are some 25 million people in America who are poor (officially defined as a household of four with less than $4,137 in annual income in 1971). If we accept that definition, we may calculate that the increase in social welfare spending over the decade of the 1960s (not the whole thing, just the **increase**) could have provided every single poor person in America with an outright gift of $4,800 annually — which means a yearly stipend of $19,200 for a family of four, or $28,800 for a welfare mother with five children.

In other words, if we had simply **given** the poor people of America this increment in social welfare spending, we could have abolished poverty outright. In fact, we could have made every family of poor people about two and a half times as wealthy as the family of the average wage-earner. Needless to remark, we have done nothing of the sort. The extra $120 billion, by and large, has not gone into the pockets of poverty families; it has gone instead into the pockets of government functionaries, consultants, and business entrepreneurs who are better off than the average American, and who promise to get more so as the scope of such activity increases.

In large measure, the regressive character of social welfare spending derives from the prominent roll assumed by public education. This has been, of course, a sacrosanct cause in American politics, and the various levels of government have vied with each other to pump out dollars for the schools. Between 1950 and 1972, spending for public schools ballooned from $5.4 billion to $45 billion — an increase of 758 percent. All of this has been done to help "the children," and since the children of the poor attend the schools, it might be assumed the result would be to benefit the impoverished.

It doesn't work out that way. There is, for one thing, rather convincing evidence that the outlay of all these billions for public education has been ineffective in improving learning skills among the poor — a point we shall be examining in more detail. There is, for another, the fact that the major recipients of the money spent for schools are school administrators and teachers, who, contrary to general impression, are well **above** the average in levels of compensation. Every increase in school spending, whatever else it does or does not do, again takes money from relatively low income citizens, the taxpayers, and bestows it on relatively high income citizens - teachers, counselors, and schools administrators.

According to *U.S. News and World Report* (September 1, 1975), the Food Stamp Program reveals a similar story.

The number of people receiving food stamps jumped from 615 thousand in 1970 to almost 20 million by mid-1975. In Puerto Rico, for example, half of the population is receiving food stamps.

It requires about 1,600 Federal employees to administer the program plus a far greater number at state and local levels.

The estimated cost of the program has escalated from a mere $14 million in 1962 to over $6 billion in 1976. That is an increase of more than 42,000 percent! You're correct — you have to pay it! Official estimates indicate an "error rate" of about 20 percent in the program — thus lax controls let too many ineligible persons into the program, while red tape keeps too many of the needy out of the program.

Carl B. Williams, Deputy U.S. Commissioner of Welfare, says, "As it now stands, the Food Stamp system is in such a mess that the Government has practically abdicated its responsibility for seeing the money gets to the needy. In effect, billions of dollars are being given away with virtually no controls."

One particularly excellent source of documentation for this orgy of government spending is a pamphlet entitled, "Significant Features Of Fiscal Federalism," a product of the Advisory Commission on Inter-Governmental Relations. This commission, created by act of Congress in 1959, is a gold mine of facts and figures.

Another fascinating source of information on "government spending gone berserk" is Donald Lambro's excellent book, *The Federal Rathole.* Most of it is devoted to only one "leak in the dike" — the more than 1,250 federal advisory boards, committees, commissions, and councils. These entities alone employ an assigned government staff of more than 4,000 people and involve an estimated 24,000 private and public citizens as participants.

In view of the fact that all of these are operated at your expense, I would like to list, at random, some of those of a more than passing interest.

Advisory Committee on Hog Cholera Eradication
Board of Tea Experts
Flue-Cured Tobacco Advisory Committee
National Advisory Board for Wild, Free-Roaming
    Horses and Burros
National Peanut Advisory Committee
Panel on Review of Laxatives, Anti-Diarrheal, Anti-Emetic,
    and Emetic Drugs
Veneral Disease Control Advisory Committee
Water-Fowl Advisory Committee
Advisory Committee on Drugs, Soaps, Cleaners, and Toilet
    Preparations
Advisory Panel on Folk Music and Jazz
Adult Development and Aging Research Committee
Advisory Committee on Women to the Secretary of Labor
Advisory Committee on the United States National Section
    Of The Inter-American Tropical Tuna Commission
Artificial Kidney — Chronic Uremia Advisory Committee
Commission on the Review of the National Policy Toward
    Gambling
Advisory Committee On Ethical and Human Value,
    Implications of Science and Technology
Advisory Panel on Dance
Advisory Panel on Drama
Advisory Panel for Genetic Biology
Anti-Infective Agents Advisory Committee
Bladder — Prostate Cancer Advisory Committee

Drug Experience Advisory Committee
Fine Arts Committee
Festive U.S.A. Program Committee
Grand Mesa National Forest Grazing Advisory Board
Lipid Metabolism Advisory Committee
South Kaibab Grazing Advisory Board
Spearfish District Grazing Advisory Board
Women's Advisory Committee on Aviation
Sleeping Bears Dunes National Lakeshore Advisory Commission
Outer Planet Science Advisory Committee
National Board for the Promotion of Rifle Practice
Music Advisory Panel

The list is endless![6]
Remember, you pay all the bills!

Any honest analysis of where your money goes requires, unfortunately, a revelation tantamount to "stepping on motherhood"! Probably the most sacrosanct of all government programs is the federal Social Security program, which has become a sacred cow.

Secretary of the Treasury William E. Simon described the situation as follows:

> Since 1935, when the Social Security Act became law, the government has tinkered with the program. Bit by bit, the soundness of its financing has been undermined. It was originally understood, at least in the way the program was presented to the public, that the premiums contributed (Social Security tax payments) would be accumulated in a reserve account, just like the pension fund of a business firm or labor union. This fund was supposed to grow steadily, earning interest, until it reached an amount large enough to meet its commitments. The contributors themselves would own the assets in the fund, for which the government would serve merely as trustee. The members' economic security in old age would be fully protected by this ownership. They would never have to depend on anyone else's charity for their livelihood.

Today, Social Security actually operates in a very different fashion. The reserve account (later relabelled the trust fund), has not been allowed to grow to more than a fraction of the required size. Instead, the government has used much of the money contributed by wage-earners to pay increased benefits to people whose contributions were not enough to warrant these benefits. The government has also failed to raise taxes commensurately with benefit increases. As a result, the trust fund is so meager that it is barely enough to keep the program going for six months. Current taxes and the fund combined are only sufficient to keep the program above water for another six years.

There is really nothing we can do about the insufficiencies of the trust fund. It is far too late to rebuild it to the required size. For that, an astonishing amount of money would be needed — by official estimates, more than two full years of our entire gross national product.

In any event, today's contributors have not been building a fund at all. The taxes they are paying into Social Security are being merely handed over as benefits to other people. In turn, when the current workers retire, they will be completely dependent upon future workers for their benefits. Their position is even more vulnerable should anything go wrong with this delicate balance. Each generation has the power through the electoral process to refuse to pay. If the next generation were to refuse to pay, the retired population would be helpless.[7]

During the last twenty years, Social Security taxes have gone up at a rate more than ten times the cost of living and, during this same period, benefits have risen less than one-third of the tax increase.

In 1940, there were 146 working contributors for every beneficiary receiving payments. By 1957, there were only six working contributors for everyone collecting benefits. Today there are only three contributors for each collecting beneficiary. Obviously a doomsday course.

On January 24th, 1976, a government advisory panel announced that the Social Security system was going broke and within a few years would be paying out more in benefits than it would be taking in. Unlike insurance companies, Social Security does not have a required reserve and, when it pays out more than it takes in, it will go broke!

In a sense, it has become a silent tax with back-breaking characteristics. In 1978, the family of four with an annual income of $12,000. to $15,000. per year began to pay more in Social Security taxes than they do in Federal Income taxes — and under current legislation that condition will worsen each year!

The notion that your employer pays half of the tax is unsound. Of necessity, every dollar paid by employers is reflected in higher prices on every product you buy or in lower take-home pay. The tax is part of his labor cost. This simply means that, in fact, you are paying the entire freight yourself!

Even more depressing is the realization that this government pension is an extremely poor investment. If the hard-earned money which you and your employer are forced to put into the current Social Security program were simply invested at 5 percent daily compounding with your bank and, at your retirement converted into an annuity, you would receive $2,010 per month for the rest of your life, which is more than three times what the current federal Social Security program will bring you!

It is particularly interesting to note that federal employees are exempt from this mandatory madness, for they are covered with most lucrative pension arrangements that we pay for! Speaking of federal employees and where your money goes, it is not surprising to discover that they are among the major beneficiaries of all this government spending. In 1955, civilian employees of the federal government made, on the average, $4,802. per year, compared to $3,959. for employees of private industry. By 1974, they had increased their average take to $14,111. per year, compared to $9,840. in the private sector.[8]

In addition, the average employee of the federal government gets approximately 50 percent more paid time off than the person working for private industry.[9]

Federal employees can retire with full pension at age 55 — a decade sooner than the typical employee in private enterprise.[10]

Probably the most expensive part of this package for you, the taxpayer, is due to a quirk in the federal pension law called the "one percent add-on." Under the federal pension system, retired federal workers receive one percent more than the increase in the cost of living each year which, under current and forseeable inflation probabilities, becomes staggering! A former member of Congress estimated that, if increases continue in the future at the same rate that they have during recent years, he will be receiving more than $17,000. per month by the end of his life expectancy!

The reader may notice that some of the horrifying statistics just encountered refer to periods ending in the mid-1970's rather than to current levels. The omissions are deliberate. Although current figures are even more terrifying, it is obvious that our difficulties are not the result of any one or two administrations (regardless of political party), but rather a trend of long standing with root causes far deeper than politics.

It would seem that the Washington establishment has achieved a magnificent formula — the more programs it can launch into being with your dollars today, the greater its increases in income after retirement from your dollars and your children's dollars tomorrow!

That's where your money goes!

"Nothing is more harmful to a new
truth than an old error."

Goethe

CHAPTER III

WHY DOES GOVERNMENT GROW?

The synergistic growth of government in the economic sphere is gravely serious. Unfortunately, history clearly indicates, as does logic, that the demise of economic freedom invariably precedes destruction of personal freedom, and with it, a collapse of responsibility and morality. Historically, that which controls or rules your economic well-being provides ever-increasing intervention into your personal liberties.

The nations whose economies are under almost total control happen to be the nations devoid of personal freedom as well.

It is interesting to note that the Soviet Constitution guarantees every personal freedom imaginable, and yet the Russian people simply do not possess what their Constitution supposedly guarantees. Why? Because economic freedom doesn't exist in the USSR. No evidence suggests that economic freedom is either the foundation of personal freedom, or at least its handmaiden. Property rights and human rights are one, in the final analysis, as are economic and personal freedom.

A rather prosaic example is the fact that a citizen of the United States was approximately 98 percent free in 1913 in the sense that he could freely decide to do whatever he wished with 98 percent of his earned income (federal taxes amounted to roughly 2 percent of his income at that time). Today that same citizen is approximately 57 percent free in the sense that he has freedom to decide the disposition of roughly that percentage of his earnings.

Do you believe in government control of earnings?

Supposedly, one of our most precious possessions is freedom of religion. Yet some Amish living in the State of Ohio suddenly found their property and livestock confiscated by federal officials. The reason? Their religion does not permit contributions to, or receipts from, the likes of a Social Security program. Hence, they found themselves searching for religious freedom in Canada. A small example, but a significant one.

Governments control people!

For example, a can of beans doesn't care what its price is. However, the people who grow the beans, the people who can the beans, the people who sell the beans, and the people who purchase the beans do care about its price. The government doesn't control wheat, but it does control the farmer's free choice as to whether or not he may grow wheat, and if so, how much. In brief, you may no longer grow what you wish to grow on your own land.[1]

Currently, some 20 million American workers must belong to labor unions whether they wish to or not, and their union dues are deducted from their paychecks through the "checkoff" before they receive them, just as if they were taxes.

Do you believe in government control over your free choice as to what organizations, clubs, or societies you wish to join — or not join?

I repeat: The only thing a government can control is people.

It is a paradox that, although our personal freedoms remain at a relatively high level, our economic freedoms are under perpetual attack and are being lost at an ever-increasing rate. If you compare highly controlled economies with less controlled economies over a significant period of time, and the answer is always the same. Where the economy is freest, there also is the highest degree of freedom of press, speech, and religion![2]

How can all of this occur when literally all of us favor individual liberty?

Thomas A. Kempis, 15th century author of *The Imitation of Christ* stated, "All men favor peace, but few men favor the things that make for peace." Perhaps a slight alteration of this observation provides the key. "All men favor individual freedom, but few men favor the things that make for individual freedom."

Why does government grow like fungus in wet weather?

Obviously there must be a great many reasons, but a few in particular deserve closer examination.

I refer to the excellent writing of Dean Russell for at least a portion of the answer:

> No one person is responsible for sapping the spirit of individualism. No one political party is to blame. The people are as responsible as the elected and appointed leaders. It is we the people who seem to have forgotten that freedom and responsibility are inseparable. It is we the people who are discarding the concept of government that brought forth the Declaration of Independence, the Constitution, and the Bill of Rights.
>
> In short, few of us seem to want to keep government out of our personal affairs and responsibilities. Many of us seem to favor various types of government-guaranteed and compulsory "security." We boast that we are responsible persons, but we vote for candidates who promise us special privileges, government pensions, government subsidies, and government electricity.
>
> Such schemes are directly contrary to the spirit of the Bill of Rights. Our heritage is being lost more through weakness than through deliberate design ... many of us are drifting back to that old concept of government that our forefathers feared and rejected. Many of us are no longer willing to accept individual responsibility for our own welfare. Yet personal freedom cannot exist without individual responsibility.

Another portion of the answer lies in what might be described as "sloppy semantics." Surely most of us wouldn't buy programs that are labelled communism, socialism, regimentation, etc. However, propose the same programs as being totally designed to help the "people" and advertise with irresistible phrases such as welfare, humanitarianism, brotherhood, security, freedom from want, social progress, and the like, and we grab the bait — hook, line and sinker!

Several years ago during a debate between Norman Thomas and William F. Buckley, Jr., Mr. Thomas stated, "I have run for President six times on the Socialist ticket and never managed to garner more than 7 percent of the popular vote. I'm happy to say, however, that almost every plank in my platform has been nailed firmly in place under legislation entitled "welfare" and "security" except medical care for the aged, and I fully expect that we'll have that very shortly."[4]

You must admire him for his forthright honesty and I'm sure his point is crystal clear.

Another aspect of government growth involves the absence of attrition. In the free market a product's success or failure is dependent upon customer acceptance. If there is no acceptance, a natural attrition takes place, and that product or that company disappears from the scene. If you and I were to set up a buggy-whip factory, there is little doubt that we would fail as there is simply no demand. However, in government, the reverse appears to be true. If a program is inefficient, or fails, there is a tendency to continually enlarge it in an effort to make it work.

Employment in the Department of Agriculture went up 47 percent between 1952 and 1972, increasing the number of employees from 78,000 to 115,000 even though the number of farms in the United States dropped by 45 percent during that same period.[5]

The point is that no attrition takes place and it is, indeed, rare that any chunk of the government bureaucracy disappears through inefficiency or because the general public simply has no need for it.

Professor Allan H. Meltzer of Carnegie Mellon University recently published a paper entitled "Why Government Grows," in which he suggests a most interesting and, in my opinion, rational theory. He suggests that in a society with a sizable middle-class and political representatives elected by popular vote, the government grows faster than the private sector whenever the costs of government can be diffused and the benefits concentrated. Such a condition creates incentive for expansion and dis-incentives for reduction in the size of government. Special interests are motivated to strongly support a program because the gain is great where the general public is either unaware of the program or, at best, sees such a diluted negative effect that they fail to resist the program. If, on the other hand, taxes were concentrated and benefits diffused, a coalition in favor of tax reduction could be organized to eliminate programs and reduce taxes.[6]

As Professor Meltzer suggests, a competitive political process sustains efficient coalitions and eliminates inefficient coalitions. Those who favor tax reduction and smaller government can be bid away — diverted and converted — by finding benefits that reward them. Such benefits include specific tax reductions, subsidies, regulation of competition, tariffs, licensing, pension plans and schooling.[7]

A free market provides an opportunity for entrepreneurs to buy inefficient businesses, improve their use, and capture the gain. The political process, on the other hand, does not offer comparable opportunities. There is little incentive to eliminate inefficiency in public enterprises, reduce the size of government, and cut taxes. The benefits achieved by such reforms are so diffuse that no person or group is highly motivated to seek such reforms.

As we have seen earlier, there is a vast redistribution of wealth from the taxpayers in general to government employees. The percentage of the labor force employed by government has increased at about the same rate as the percentage of income paid in taxes. Both have doubled and redoubled in this century.[8]

Perhaps the best explanation for the phenomenal growth of government is ignorance. The American public has not been exposed on any broad scale to the principles imperative to a free society. This can be primarily traced to a complete lack in this area of primary knowledge within our educational system.

The philosophy of an education system and the philosophy of a nation reflect one another.

It is logical to assume that the philosophy of an educational system would reflect, to a great extent, the philosophy of the teachers involved in it. It would seem equally reasonable to suspect that the philosophy of teachers, per se, might be traced directly to the teachers of teachers.

Although there are, and have been, many members of the "teachers of teachers" club, I would like to mention but five: Dr. Harold Rugg, Dr. George S. Counts, Dr. William Kilpatrick, Dr. John Dewey and Dr. James E. Mendenhill. Four of these gentlemen were officers of the Intercollegiate Society for Socialism. Four were graduates of Columbia University's Teacher College. These men must be classified as architects of the wave of "progressive education" that swept our nation during the '30's and '40's, and only now is beginning to subside. These men must be regarded as the leading "teachers of teachers." Collectively, they authored almost two hundred books and teachers guides on education, and complete Social Science courses. An estimated ten million students and teachers have used their material.

Their writings share a basic viewpoint, which can be summed up in the following points:

1. In education for a new social order, we must teach what to think, not how to think.

2. The American system must be regarded as a failure.

3. We must eliminate the possibility of failure and strive for equalization and conformity for the new social order.

4. Standards of excellence have no place in the new social order.

Dr. Harold Rugg authored a number of major books, the best known being *The Great Technology* published in 1933. In it he states, "Our task is nothing short of questioning the whole philosophy of living, the philosophy of private capitalism and laissez faire."

Elsewhere in the book he says that:

"We must uproot the deep-rooted loyalties of the American people to an entire culture lacking in integrity."

"It is clear, therefore, that if educational agencies are to be utilized in the production of a new social order, an indispensible first step is that of developing a totally new outlook upon life and education among the rank and file of teachers."

He refers to the founding fathers of the United States and basic American history this way:

"Nothing about this story of degradation is clearer than that, in any of those decades, a fairly decent standard of living could have been had by the peoples of the expanding west. That it was not, and is not today, can be traced primarily to the theory and practice of government set up by our fathers."

In one of his pamphlets entitled "Building A Science Of Society For The Schools," Dr. Rugg suggested, "A new public mind is to be created. How? Only by creating tens of millions of individual minds and welding them into a new social mind. That is the task of the building of a science of society for the school."

The titles on some of Dr. Rugg's other books might be of some interest.

Building A Science Of Society For The Schools
Social Reconstruction
Conquest Of America
The Soviet Challenge To America

In addition, this prolific author put together fourteen textbooks, eight for elementary grades and six for junior high school.

Rugg and Mendenhall collaborated on a number of teacher's guides comprising what was called the Rugg Mendenhall System. In these the teacher is given the required answers to the posed questions and is instructed how to interpret historical facts and other material in the textbooks. Examples:

"Is the United States a land of opportunity for all our people? Why? Answer: The United States is not a land of opportunity for all our people; for one-fifth of the people do not earn any money at all. There are great differences in the standards of living of the different classes of people. The majority do not have any real security."

"Treat the War for Independence essentially as an economic struggle between the ruling classes of England and the Colonies."[9]

Jenkin Lloyd Jones, editor of the *Tulsa Tribune*, delivered the following comments on the subject a few years ago at a meeting of the American Society of Newspaper Editors.

We are now at the end of the third decade of the national insanity known as "progressive education." This is the education where everybody passes, where the report cards are noncommittal lest the failer be faced with the fact of his failure, where all move at a snail's pace like a trans-Atlantic convoy so that the slowest need not be left behind, and all proceed toward adulthood in the lockstep of "togetherness."

With what results? At an age when European kids are studying the human capillary system, our youngsters are raising pollywogs on the classroom windowsill and pretending to keep store. This is what is known as "learning by doing." We have produced tens of thousands of high school graduates who move their lips as they read and cannot write a coherent paragraph. While our Russian contemporaries, who were supposed to be dedicated to the mass man, have been busy constructing an elite, we have been engaged in the wholesale production of mediocrity. What a switch!

I wish you could have read all the letters I have received in the past few months from disgusted teachers who have tried to re-introduce principles of hard work and integrity in their classrooms over the opposition of the school hierarchies. It is high time that these Ph.D poobahs of John Deweyism stepped forward and permitted themselves to be graded. But no.[10]

Dr. Max Rafferty, former head of the California school system and controversial author of *Suffer, Little Children,* offers some equally scathing comments on American education.

The great wheel of history has turned ponderously full-circle since the Punic Wars. A happier time for children dawned a century ago, and in that Golden Age, a whole new pantheon of youthful gods and goddesses came down from Mount Olympus and made old Earth a magic place for boys and girls.

Wilfred and Ivanhoe rode stirrup to stirrup with Couer de Leon, and the evil hold of Torquilstone burned eternal witness to the power of youth and goodness. Laughing and shouting in the same great company rose Arthur with his Table Round, forever splintering their lances in the cause of right... roistering and invincible swaggered Porthos, Athos and Aramis, with the young D'Artagnan, ever ready to draw those magic blades, the wonder of the world, for truth and glory and the queen. The horn of Roland echoed through the pass at Roncesvalles...

Were not these fit gods for the children of mankind?

Apart and in a merry company leaped and played the Child Immortals. Hand in hand the longhaired Alice walked Christopher Robin, bright eyes alert for talking to rabbits and greedy little bears. Sturdy Jim Hawkins counted his pieces of eight... while young Tom Sawyer kept a wary lookout for the menace that was Injun Joe.

When in any age have children had such shining exemplars?

Hansel and Gretel have been dehydrated and neutralized to the status of Cincinnati children on a Sunday-school picnic, and Jack the Giant-Killer to a schoolboy swatting flies. Everything that was fearful and wonderful and glamorous has been leveled off to the lowest common denominator.

Ulysses and Penelope have been replaced by Dick and Jane in the textbooks of our schools. The quest for the Golden Fleece has been crowded out by the visit of Tom and Susan to the zoo. Jackie pursues his insipid goal of a ride in the district garbage truck with good old crotchety Mr. Jones while the deathless ride of Paul Revere goes unwept, unhonored and unsung. It is interesting, and certainly significant, that modern education has deliberately debunked the hero to make room for the jerk. The lofty exception to the rank and file, whom all of us could envy and emulate, has been compelled to give way to the Great Mediocrity, the synthesis of all that is harmless and safe and banal among us.

Watch the abler ones grow dull and apathetic, bored and lackluster, as they yawn and watch the clock over the stupid adventures of Muk-Muk, the Eskimo Boy, or Little Pedro from Argentina. Then, suddenly, as though opening an enchanted window upon a radiant pageant, give them the story of the wrath of Achilles. Let them stand with Casabanca upon a burning deck. Trek with them in spirit to the Yukon, and . . . place them upon the shot-swept shrouds of Bonhomme Richard, and let them thrill to those words flashing like a rapier out of the past, "I have not yet begun to fight." Kneel with them behind the cotton bales at New Orleans with Andy Jackson at their side as the redcoats begin to emerge from the mist of the Louisiana swamps and the sullen guns of Lafitte begin to pound. Watch their faces.[11]

It is most certainly true, on the one hand, that the sudden and unexpected appearance of Sputnik I in 1957 shook the educational world right down to its shoelaces and caused considerable re-evaluation which, in its wake, washed out much of the "progressive education" myth. It is just as true that much of its philosophy remains and that it will probably take at least three generations to phase out its effects. Still another part of the picture is the constantly growing activity of the federal government in the educational area through Federal Aid to Education. Who pays the piper calls the tune. The United States Supreme Court stated it well in its Wickard vs. Fulburn decision in October 1942. "It is hardly lack of due process for the government to regulate that which it subsidizes."

This decision must have come as a surprise to many Americans who had failed to realize that they could not have both local control of schools and subsidies. It is indeed difficult for one to be concurrently dependent and independent.

There is little doubt that an educational system that has, for more than three generations, negated the moral principles involved in our Nation's heritage and, for whatever reason, sewn the seeds of neglect and added the fertilizer that has achieved quantum jumps in the size of government.

"I believe it is better to tell the truth than a lie. I believe it is better to be free than to be a slave. I believe it is better to know than to be ignorant."

H. L. Mencken

CHAPTER IV

"THE TROUBLE WITH PEOPLE..."

It was Josh Billings, the American humorist, who said, "The trouble with people ain't ignorance, it's what they know that ain't so." There is an unusual amount of common sense contained in that statement.

In order to put the trends of the past forty years into sensible perspective, a basic understanding of capitalism and how and why it functions is essential. We will examine some of those things "we know that ain't so" in order to dispel faulty notions.

Here are the myths relating to our market economy:

Myth No. 1 — Capitalism favors the rich.
Myth No. 2 — Socialism favors the poor.
Myth No. 3 — Wealth is limited and, therefore, should be divided as evenly as possible.
Myth No. 4 — Management and labor have conflicting interests and are, therefore, natural antagonists.

Myth No. 5 — Labor unions are primarily responsible for the economic gains and
high standard of living of the
American people.

Myth No. 6 — One man's economic gain is reflected
by another man's economic loss.

Myth No. 7 — High profits are unconscionable and
contrary to the best interests of the
working class.

These first seven mythical assumptions are primarily
economic in nature and are best dealt with as a group. The
interlocking nature of the principles involved makes this form
of rebuttal easier to understand.

It is evident that self-interest is, of necessity, the primary
motivation in human behavior. With this thought in mind, let
us take a look at the function of capital and why we call our
system Capitalism.

Throughout the world, since history began, nations have
tried to redistribute the existing economic pie with little or no
success. All "command" systems are based on the assumption
that the amount of economic wealth is fixed. Therefore, their
preoccupation has been with how goods are distributed and **not**
with how they are produced. The genius in the American idea
has been to simply bake continuously bigger and bigger pies
so that an ever-increasing segment of the population can
prosper.

Capital has been the heart of the phenomenal economic
growth in the United States over the past 150 years, as well
as the primary creator of a living standard that became the
highest in the world.

Today a man can leave his home in New York City and arrive at his destination in San Francisco in less than six hours.
The reason he can do so is that he is able to utilize probably
five to ten billion dollars in capital that has been created, accumulated, and invested in the taxicabs he used to reach the
airport, the super-highways over which he traveled, extensive
airport facilities, the 747 jumbo-jet, and all of the luxuries that
accompany it.

Less than 150 years ago, it took a traveler approximately 200 extremely uncomfortable days to go from New York to San Francisco and involved probably only a few hundred dollars in capital in terms of his Conestoga wagon, horses, and allied equipment. **There is no job that can be done manually any faster today than it was done 200 years ago.** It is not possible for a man to earn more than a few dollars an hour for moving earth with a shovel (even if he belongs to a union), but if someone will provide the capital required to furnish him with a three cubic yard caterpillar tractor, he then can earn $10 to $15 per hour — and that is where our prosperity arises.

I am not against voluntary unionism for those who feel more secure within its embrace, but to suggest that the labor union is the **primary** source of our improved standard of living is ludicrous. We had the highest wage rates in the world in the United States in 1911, many years before the labor union movement took shape in the United States. The simple fact is that *tools have created the increased productivity for almost every working man and those tools are a consequence of accumulated capital.*

This position is adequately supported by noting that, in the United States, the average job requires almost $40,000 in capital whereas, in Europe, the average job is capitalized at approximately $20,000. The figure for the Soviet Union is far less than that (and the Soviet Union still has to utilize more than 45 percent of its population on the farms in order to feed itself). In most of the third world (Africa et al), the capital provided per worker is approximately $1,000.

What are the sources of this capital that has provided the spark that makes our system far more productive than any other? There are essentially only two. One is that bugaboo known as corporate profits and the other is private savings. (It is interesting to note that for some time we have double-taxed corporate profits as well as single-taxed the interest on private savings — hardly the most inspiring way to encourage the creation of capital.)

Therefore, as economist Peter Drucker puts it, "profit is primarily nothing more than the cost of additonal capital with which to provide more and better tools with which to increase the productivity and earnings of everyone who works." The phenomenal increases in our gross national product over the past hundred and fifty years are graphic evidence that our system has continued to increase dramatically the size of the "economic pie" by creating a system that functions for the benefit of all who are willing or able to work.

A more realistic description of what the typical American business consists of might be much in order at this point. There is a tendency to think of "business" as Caterpillar Tractor, General Motors, Westinghouse, Xerox, I.B.M., 3-M, and so on. Most businesses begin with a few individuals, whether they be a Ford Motor Company or a General Motors. Today, approximately 95 out of every 100 producing businesses in the United States have fewer than 100 employees, and almost 31 percent have fewer than 20 employees. Most of these businesses are either majority or totally owned by the same individual or individuals that manage them. As for the publicly-held corporations — they embrace an ownership of more than 30 million stockholders (more than one-third of all the people working in the United States).

The typical American corporation, according to the Department of Commerce, paid out taxes in an amount more than three times that paid out in dividends to the owners — and then the owners are, of course, taxed again on the dividends. In this typical corporation, employee compensation generally runs 19 times the amount paid to the stockholder-owners. A man going in business says, in effect, "I will furnish all the capital required, jobs for new employees, and raw materials from the far corners of the world. I will devise saleable products and advertise them, sell them, do the accounting, pay the taxes and all other operating expenses, pay the employees 90 percent of the dollars that are left, and assume all of the risk." A good percentage of his profit (and he takes a high risk of loss) becomes simply the cost of additional capital investment with which to provide more jobs and buy productivity.

Labor and management are, in fact, a team in that neither can work without the other and both are productive. There is some question, however, as to whether all of the taxes paid personally by the people who work at both management and labor levels, as well as those taxes paid by the Corporation, are employed productively.

The evidence is overwhelming: Capitalism benefits more segments of our population than any other system. All other systems tend to benefit only those in power.

There is no limit to the wealth that can be generated in society. Labor and management are partners and there is no such thing as "unconscionable profits," because profits benefit them all. In a free-market system, one man's gain is generally another man's gain, for his economic well-being creates additional investment capital for research and development, new products, jobs and all that goes with it. To suggest otherwise is tantamount to the proposition that illness is caused by the healthy.

Myth No. 8 — The Robber Baron Myth

Throughout your school years, your history textbooks and most of your teachers, continuously emphasized that the nineteenth century in the United States was a time of unrestrained individualism highlighted by heartless capitalists who exploited the poor and helpless with profit as their only motive.

We were taught that the rich got richer and totally at the expense of the poor and downtrodden.

While the nineteenth century was, indeed, a period of rugged individualism, almost every other aspect of the myth is false. There were indeed some rapacious entrepreneurs in that period. But there is probably no other period in human history during which the ordinary working-man experienced such unprecedented improvement in his standard of living as the one from 1865 to 1920 — the same period when unrestrained individualism dominated the American scene. The evidence is incontrovertible, not only in the statistics that economists have constructed demonstrating the drastic rises in national income, but also in the numbers of people who flocked eagerly to the United States during that period.

The notion that people flocked to this country to be worse off makes no sense. Did they come here to find less freedom and poorer economic circumstances? There is no more dramatic way in which people can vote than with their feet.

The historical truth is that this period of alleged monopolistic and heartless capitalist cruelty was a time of immense generosity and charity. The period of unrestrained individualism was a period when nonprofit community hospitals and libraries were first established and developed. It was the time that great philanthropic activity was initiated by America's leading industrial families. It was the period when scores of colleges were founded throughout the country.

Myth No. 9 — The Great Depression was caused by the failure of the private enterprise system.

Nobel Laureate Dr. Milton Friedman expresses this rebuttal as well as anyone:

Somehow people believed that the Great Depression occurred because private enterprise could not organize society properly, that it was necessary for government to step in in order to save society, that the New Deal and all that followed was a necessary corrective to the mistakes and disasters produced by the deficiencies of private enterprise and unbridled competition.

The only trouble with these beliefs is that they are completely wrong. The elementary truth is that the Great Depression was produced by government mismanagement. It was not produced by the failure of private enterprise, it was produced by the failure of government to perform a function which had been widely assigned to it. Since time immemorial, government has been granted the function, wisely or not, of controlling the monetary system. In our Constitution government is given the power to coin money and determine the value thereof.

The reason we had the Great Depression was because government failed in that task. In 1914 we had a supposedly great reform. I say 'reform,' but I would like to put that in quotes because experience shows that not all reforms are improvements. In this particular case the great 'reform' was the establishment of a Federal Reserve System, the establishment of a central banking system. It was established supposedly to prevent what where called banking panics.[1]

The Federal Reserve System actually created bank failures (rather than preventing them) by failing to act during the period from 1929 to 1933. During the year preceding December of 1930, when the Bank of the United States failed, nothing more than a recessionary adjustment had been taking place. The collapse of the Bank of the United States triggered runs on banks throughout the country and the Federal Reserve System failed to back up the banks in meeting the demands of their customers. The result? Countless banks failed throughout the country and in March of 1933 all banks in the United States were closed (including the Federal Reserve Banks) for several days, creating the worst and most disastrous panic in American history.

One-third of all of the banks in the United States failed between 1929 and 1933 and the money supply fell by one-third. That the disaster was preventable, had proper actions been taken by the Federal Reserve System, is clearly documented.

How did the "great depression" myth become so entrenched? Human nature decrees that one would prefer taking credit for good happenings and pass the blame for unpleasant occurrences on to others. Government agencies by their very nature congratulate themselves publically during strong economic times and condemn the private sector or "events beyond our control" when difficulties ensue.

The important fact is that the Great Depression is a classic example of the inability of centralized government to direct and control economic affairs with any degree of success, **not** historical evidence of free enterprise instability. Frankly, it is my belief that if the Federal Reserve System had not been created some 15 years earlier, the economic debacle would have been avoided in the first place.

> Myth No. 10 — Government can spend money at nobody's expense.

The French economist, Frederic Bastiat, defined government

as that fiction whereby everybody believes that he can live at the expense of everybody else.

The general acceptance of the idea that it is possible to spend money with nobody paying for it is difficult to understand. There exists a constant and seemingly endless demand for more and larger government programs. Where are we going to raise the money? The normal response is "tax business." But business corporations really don't pay any taxes. They are extracted from customers, stockholders (owners) and employees. Unlike the federal government, the businessman doesn't have a printing press in his basement, and the only way he can pay money to the government is by imposing a burden on somebody through higher prices, lower wages, or lower dividends.

> Myth No. 11 — Government spends money to benefit the poor at the expense of the rich.

This is a myth which is promoted by those who believe in mandatory rather than voluntary charity. This belief provides the foundation for welfarism. We are all in favor of helping the poor, provided they are being helped with someone else's money or you and I are defined as poor. Economist Milton Friedman records his impressions of a summit conference that President Ford called in Washington:

> I was very amused by the parade of special interests who came up to the platform, and one after another said, "it is absolutely essential that we cut the government budget to beat inflation. I will tell you how to cut the government budget: spend more on me." The elementary fact is that almost all government programs are either a complete waste and help nobody, or they benefit the middle and upper classes at the expense of both the very poor and the very rich. That proposition would itself be the subject matter for a longer talk than I have so far given, so I only want to illustrate it with a few examples to show you that it is not entirely a demagogic statement but has some backing. Consider the case I mentioned earlier — Social Security. That's

a program that is widely regarded as helping the poor at the expense of the middle and upper income classes. The facts are, first of all, that the tax which finances Social Security is the most regressive tax in our tax system. It's a payroll tax on wages up to a maximum, the reverse of what is regarded as a graduated tax. The benefits are related hardly at all to the amount of taxes anybody has paid and, in any event, are to a large extent inequitable. A man who has a million dollars income a year from securities will receive his full Social Security benefit after age 65. But if between age 65 and 72 he should work, and gets his income from labor, then not only doesn't he get any benefits if he earns more than a modest amount, but he also has to pay additional taxes on the wages he earns. Much more fundamentally, the young men from poorer families, the people who are going to be poor in our society, go to work and start paying Social Security taxes at the age of 16 and 17. People who are going to be in the upper classes or upper middle classes go to college and graduate school; they don't start paying Social Security taxes until age 24, 25 or 26. On the other side of the picture, it is a well-known demographic fact that richer people live longer than poorer people, and so they will receive Social Security 'benefits' for more years. In other words, **the poor fellow at the bottom has been suckered into paying taxes for more years in order to provide better-off people with benefits for more years,** and that's what's known as a program helping the poor at the expense of the rich.[2]

Myth No. 12 — Inflation is high prices.

To quote William F. Rickenbacker, that is like saying "flood causes torrential rains."

Inflation is a cause, not an effect! During the last six years the Federal Government has spent one hundred and fifty one billion dollars more than it received in taxes. In order to pay the bills it ran the printing presses to create the additional funds necessary. It's interesting to note that deficits have occurred every year from 1961 through 1976. (The exception is 1969, in which there was a modest 3.2 billion dollar surplus.) The best way to describe this phenomenon would be to suggest that if you were involved in a Monopoly game in your living room and excused yourself to go into the bedroom and remove all the play money from a second Monopoly game in the closet, and then brought it back into the living room and introduced it into your game, the results would be obvious. No additional hotels, no additional houses, no additional Marvin Gardens, Park Places, or Boardwalks — just double the money supply. The results? The prices double!

In 1946 the money supply in the United States was approximately 100 billion dollars. Since then, we have printed enough counterfeit money to triple the money supply and it now rests at almost 300 billion dollars. *That is inflation. It is created only at the federal level. It is the primary cause of high prices.*

It is true that large wage settlements with unions, increase in the prices of raw materials, and a multitude of other costs, (including rising Social Security requirements) add to the prices of products.

It has been estimated by leading economists that the cost of the governmental regulatory agencies such as O.S.H.A., E.P.A., et al, added more than 100 billion dollars to consumer prices during the year 1975! That's close to $500 per person, or $2,000 in extra costs for a family of four.

Nonetheless, "running the printing presses" is probably responsible for a minimum of 75 to 80 percent of all price increases.

> Myth No. 13 — We don't have to worry about the national debt because we owe it to ourselves.

In 1975 alone the interest on the debt reached approximately 45 billion dollars. If that debt created by deficit spending didn't exist, we would have the choice of either cutting individual taxes by 29 percent, corporate taxes by 90 percent, or Social Security taxes by 27 percent. By any measurement, that is expensive!

The federal debt is largely owed to the Federal Reserve Banks, the International Monetary Fund, and private citizens who hold Federal bonds and notes. That's a lot different than saying we owe it to ourselves.

"Government can't give us anything
without depriving us of something
else."

Henry Hazlitt

CHAPTER V

THE TRANSFER SOCIETY

All of this has served to create what might best be described
as *the transfer or interventionist system.*

If one is to understand any of what is happening, he must
have some concept of the underpinnings involved in the creation of the transfer society.

The transfer theory is as time-worn as the history of man,
and it simply involves the redistribution of income and wealth
with the intent to level everyone, rather than equality of opportunity. Essentially the transfer proposition involves three
states — each stage developing from the one that precedes it.

The first stage simply involves the idea that you can take
from the rich and give to the poor through the political system.
It is particularly significant in this stage to evaluate the
promise as contrasted to the performance. As an example, if
the Federal government had confiscated 100 percent of the
personal income of all millionaires in the United States during
the year 1974 (millionaires being defined as anyone with a net
worth of over one million dollars), all of the money collected
would have run the Federal establishment for approximately
30 hours.[1]

Of even greater impact is the realization that if the Federal
government had confiscated all annual income over $32,000,

the additional revenue collected would total approximately 12.8 billion dollars — enough to run the Federal establishment for eleven and one-half days![2]

It is obvious that the well-to-do are so few that the theft of their money would have little impact on taxes or government.

In the case of the United States, the first stage of the transfer society was launched approximately in 1930 and for all practical purposes, ran out of gas about 1959 with the political realization that additional raises in basic taxes were simply out of the question.

The second stage required attacking the income and wealth of the middle class and was engineered through deficit spending and the resulting inflation. This, of course, collapsed the value of savings, bonds, etc. The consequences of stage two are that debtors are gaining and creditors are losing through inflation which creates a transfer of assets through the inflationary consequences.

At 10 percent annual inflation the transfer of income reaches approximately 300 billion dollars per year from the economic middle class to the various special interests that we have previously discussed.

In short, society proceeds to live off the savings of the middle class, thus destroying it in the process. It is not the rich but the approximately 90 percent of the American workers who earn between $10,000 and $30,000 annually who are supporting the massive government programs involving Welfare, Social Security, Food Stamps, etc., and it is, indeed, consuming their very substance.[3]

In terms of the United States, we entered the second phase in approximately the year 1960, and we have moved, at an ever accelerating pace, into the third stage of the transfer system.

This final stage involves stealing or consuming capital through government borrowing and inflation which essentially proceeds to destroy the sources of productivity.

If the consequences of this policy were only economic it would be bad enough but, as indicated earlier, the demise of economic freedom invariably precedes the destruction of personal freedom, and with it, a collapse of responsibility and morality. We have taken a look at the condition of our economic freedom; we have glanced at the embryo effects upon our personal freedom; and the last ten years have given us convincing evidence of its effects upon our responsibility and morality.

The riots of the late 1960s, both on the college campuses and in the streets; the ever increasing crime rate, particularly of the violent category; and the collapse of personal standards of integrity demonstrate the potential disaster.

In the face of this collapse of responsibility and morality did we hear the condemnation expected from high places? Hardly. Rather we hear:

"In the great struggle to advance civil and human rights . . . even a jail sentence is no longer a dishonor but a proud achievement."[4]

"The old code of equity law under which we live commands for every wrong a remedy, but in too many communities, in too many parts of the country, wrongs are inflicted on Negro citizens for which there are no remedies at law. Unless the Congress acts, their only remedy is in the street."[5]

"We must take from the haves and give to the havenots."[6]

In the face of violence and chaos, let us once again recall the words of the Supreme Court in the Durand vs. Hollins decision in the year 1860.

"The great object and duty of government is the protection of lives, liberty and property of the people composing it, whether abroad or at home, and any government failing in the accomplishment of that objective, or the performance of that duty is not worth preserving."

To quote the work of M. Stanton Evans, "It is therefore curious to note that, while government today is taking functions never remotely envisioned for it by America's founders . . . it seems increasingly unable to handle the most elementary tasks of civil authority."[7]

It would, indeed, appear that the circle of principle is self-proving. Freedom can only exist in the presence of responsibility, and responsibility is the by-product of morality. Morality cannot exist without self-discipline, and self-discipline is required in order to have freedom and around and around it goes, as unbending as the law of gravity.

"When men are most sure and arrogant they are commonly most mistaken."

David Hume

CHAPTER VI

THE FLIGHT FROM REALITY

Most of the history of mankind demonstrates that poverty, famine and deprivation were taken for granted as a way of life for all but the most fortunate on this earth — and the reasons for the condition are clear.

For centuries the only pertinent discussion was centered around **which** form of authoritarianism should prevail — thoughts of personal liberty for all weren't even considered.

The Age of Capitalism didn't begin until the 1800s. It was preceded by one form of Command System after another:

Age of Mercantilism   1500 - 1800 AD
Age of Feudalism   500 - 1500 AD
Age of Military Socialism   300 - 500 AD

Up until very recently, most people were serfs. And, but for Adam Smith, Jeremy Bentham, David Hume, John Locke and their colleagues, we too would be enjoying serfdom.

During the early 1900s the United States set forth on a new course — a mixed system involving some aspects of a free market combined with increasing government intervention. This has led us into what can only be described as radical interventionism.

Americans consume more because they produce more, but the interventionist mentality has little interest in how goods are produced — only how they are distributed. To suggest that the free market functions contrary to the interests of the poor is to reveal one's ignorance. All evidence indicates that no other system has done so much to wipe out poverty. A free economy is not like a poker game in that one man's stack of chips must go down in order that another's might go up. In a free economy — *all stacks grow!*

Nobel laureate Dr. Friedrich A. Von Hayek has probably expressed this truth as well as anyone:

> There is one supreme myth which more than any other has served to discredit the economic system to which we owe our present day civilization. It is the legend of the deterioration of the position of the working classes in consequence of the rise of "Capitalism" or the "Industrial System."
>
> The wide-spread emotional aversion to "Capitalism" is closely connected with this belief that the undeniable growth of wealth which the competitive order had produced was purchased at the price of depressing the standard of life of the weakest elements of society. A more careful examination of the facts has, however, led to a thorough refutation of this belief.
>
> The freedom of economic activity which in England had proved so favorable to the rapid growth of wealth was probably in the first instance an almost accidental by-product of the limitations which the revolution of the 17th century had placed on the powers of government; and only after its beneficial effects had come to be widely noticed did the economists later undertake the connection and to argue for the removal of remaining barriers to commercial freedom. We use the term Capitalism here because it is the most familiar name, but only with great reluctance, since with its modern connotations it is itself largely the creation of that socialistic interpretation of economic history with which we are concerned. The term is especially misleading when, as is often the case, it is connected with the idea of the rise of the propertyless proletariat,

which by some devious process has been deprived of their rightful ownership of the tools of their work.[1]

The historical truth is, the connection between Capitalism and the rise of the proletariat hardly supports the theory alleging the expropriation of the masses. Prior to the industrial revolution and the rise of Capitalism, history records a continuing surplus of population doomed to early death. This is supported by the fact that population levels that had been stationary for centuries began to increase rapidly. The proletariat which Capitalism theoretically created was not a proportion of the population that had existed before; rather it was an additional population blessed by the new opportunities of employment provided by the industrial revolution.

It was the first time in history that people found it in their interest to use their earnings to provide new instruments of production to be operated by others who, without them, could not have produced adequately to survive.

The increases in personal well-being and personal wealth raised aspirations as rapidly as they raised the standard of living and the coming middle class began to emerge.

Economic suffering that had always existed became more conspicuous because the general wealth was increasing so rapidly and, although there is evidence that misery existed, there is none that it was anywhere near as great as it had been before. General health, on the whole, was benefited rather than harmed.

It was during this period that the labor displacement myth emerged — the theory that the introduction of machinery would produce a general reduction in demand for labor. Though on the face of it, it would seem to be a logical conclusion, all historical fact and statistical documentation even to today demonstrate that precisely the opposite has taken place. It is true that workers were moved from one section in a manufacturing operation to another, or in some cases, were forced to move from one company to another, but the overall consequence was a great increase in the number of employed and the opportunity provided to almost all of them

Of course there were labor displacements and specific cases

of great hardship, but that cannot color the fact that the general results were almost an economic miracle.

Unfortunately, the public perception of business is, indeed, a classic example of a flight from reality. In almost every respect the "public's notions" bear little similarity to the facts.

1. Of more than 3 million American businesses, only 12,169 can be classified as "big," that is, employing more than 500 people. Therefore, less than one-half of one percent of all the businesses in the United States are "big."

2. All of these "big" businesses combined employ less than 20 percent of our total work force.

3. Approximately 5 percent of America's wealth in terms of property, plants, equipment, and inventory is held by U.S. manufacturing corporations with assets of one billion dollars or more.

4. There is a tendency to believe that "big business" is born full-grown and in a position to snuff out little competitors and run roughshod over consumers. The truth is that almost all businessess begin their lives as a **very** small entity with only a few employees. John Hertz's little car rental lot in Chicago, Roland H. Macy's drygoods store in New York, Ford Motor Company, 3-M, and others, are typical examples, and they became "big business" simply because the American public liked and bought their product or service. Some products such as steel, automobiles, chemicals, petroleum, tractors, etc. require a scale of investment that is beyond the reach of the "ma and pa enterprise," and grow because investors vote with their dollars and fulfill the requirements of the American public in that fashion.

5. Those few companies that do become large, however, in a very real way create thousands of small companies to serve their needs. 3-M, for example, uses products and services from more than 30,000 small businesses. Hewlett-Packard deals with more than 6,000 small American companies and Cater-

pillar Tractor, General Motors, General Electric, Xerox and I.B.M. function in precisely the same way — and in doing so provide, directly or indirectly, millions of jobs for American workers.

6. The idea that large companies can exert "monopoly control" in their field of endeavor is less than realistic. General Motors may account for approximately 43 percent of the U.S. auto sales, but it has only 22 percent of the world market. In spite of the massive investment required in the energy field by the oil producers, there isn't a single company with more than 10 percent of the total market. U.S. Steel, though a domestic giant, competes not only against its domestic counterparts, but has real difficulty competing against the world's largest steel maker, Japan's Nippon Steel. Such is the case in almost every product requiring heavy investment.

7. In spite of the effects of inflation, large union wage settlements, etc., American industry never ceases to demonstrate its ingenuity. Twenty years ago, an eleven cubic-foot refrigerator cost over $500.00 and today you can buy a twenty-one cubic foot model complete with freezer, automatic ice-maker, etc., for much less. The electronic calculator on my desk cost $250.00 just a few years ago, and today can be purchased for $49.95. The 27" color television set in your living room cost less than the early 10" and 12" black and white sets of 20 years ago. Today you can purchase a 10,000 BTU room air conditioner for under $200.00. Twenty years ago a similar unit would require almost twice as much electrical power and was priced at over $400.00. The electric drill that cost $20.00 in 1958 can today be purchased for approximately $12.00. Such a list of the achievements of American industry could continue for pages.[2]

8. When the automobile was first produced it was assumed that it would be available only to the very wealthy. Only the dreams and ingenuity of Amer-

ican industrialists made it possible to produce it for the masses. Even a simple item such as ladies' hosiery was originally created for the "wealthy few" and today it covers the beautiful legs of almost every woman in America and we might all agree that it has become a delightful everyday necessity.

9. In spite of the above facts, we hear constant reference to the "power of the big corporation." Of course a corporation has power. Keep in mind, however, that a corporation cannot *force* you to do anything but must rely on a free market. A government can deprive you of your life, your liberty, or your property. It can arrest you, put you in jail, take your money by force, or inflate the currency.[3]

One ought to be able to assume that the business community, as the productive muscle of the American economy, would be at the forefront of efforts to confine the fiasco of geometric government growth and intervention. Unfortunately, such is not the case!

Incongruous though it may seem, those who argue that "big business" does, in fact, use coercion and government for its own ends are, at least, partially correct.

In order to understand this phenomenon, it is important to recognize that government, as it is practiced today, is an influence system. It is the uniting of some business interests with the power and influence of government that creates the problem. A business entity cannot **force** you to do anything unless it has managed to "arrange with government" to deny competitors the right to serve the marketplace, control prices, erect tariff barriers, or in general create benefits at the expense of other businesses and the consumer. The businesses that do so employ political clout the way the labor unions do, or members of the academic and foundation world, or (as indicated earlier) members of the government establishment itself.[4]

The percentage of businessmen involved in this type of activity is very small. But there are far too many who lobby in Washington, D.C., seeking an edge for themselves, or agency harrassment for their competition, or a high tariff to keep those foreign goods out.

Government influence and power is an essential ingredient in order to sustain a monopoly!

It is particularly interesting to note that most of this activity takes place in those industries where regulatory agencies have been established to "help the consumer" (transportation, communications, energy, etc.). Typically, in fact, they do precisely the opposite. For a delightfully penetrating examination of the fact that "most government bureaus and regulatory agencies tend to accomplish precisely the reverse of their original intentions" see Dr. Milton Friedman's *Capitalism and Freedom.*[5]

Classic examples of this kind of activity are referred to in Congressman Philip M. Crane's book, *The Sum of Good Government,* as follows:

> In an unusual statement for a federal official, F.T.C. Chairman Lewis A. Engman attacked federal regulatory agencies — specifically mentioning the Civil Aeronautics Board and the Interstate Commerce commission — as being protective of industries they regulate in an unhealthy relationship that unnecessarily raises costs to the consumer and contributes to inflation.
>
> Engman declared, "Most regulated industries have become federal protectorates, living in a cozy world of cost-plus, safely protected from the ugly specter of competition, efficiency and innovation." To correct these problems he called for re-examination of "every regulation or regulatory policy that contributes to inflation."
>
> The failure of government regulatory agencies is something that has recently become a reality accepted as true even by the strongest proponents of such bodies.
>
> Consider, for example, the record of the Civil Aeronautics Board. Professors Peter Passell and Leonard Ross of Columbia University write that "economic estimates suggest that, without the Civil Aeronautics Board, you could fly from New York to Los Angeles for $95.00 and from Washington, D.C. to Chicago for

$33.00. Current fares of the two runs are $275.00 and $120.00 respectively. In general, it seems clear that, without the C.A.B., air fares could be considerably lower throughout the United States and abroad.

Rather than thrust the question of air fares to the marketplace, Passell and Ross suggest that "Congress set up independent regulatory commissions with bipartisan membership and lengthy terms . . . (that would) preside over 10 percent of the national economy, including interstate railway, truck, barge and ship transportation; communications by telephone, cable, radio and television; electric and atomic power; banking, the stock market and cattle investment trusts."

No interstate airline can operate without a certificate from the C.A.B. declaring its "public interest, convenience and necessity." This means that no one can enter the airline business unless the C.A.B. decides that the "public interest" requires it. Interestingly, since it was established in 1938, the C.A.B. has yet to find that the "public interest" would be served by the entry of a single new competitor to the ten major airlines.[6]

Aviation Week magazine points out that the direct operating costs of a 747 are approximately one cent per seat mile, or about $25.00 from New York to Los Angeles. Professor Michael E. Livine, a former C.A.B. staff member, regards that as significant evidence that "the board has . . . operated an imperfect cartel for the benefit of the industry." Professors Passell and Ross feel that the answer to high air fares and lack of competition is the allowance of free competition and abolishment of the C.A.B.'s power to fix minimum prices and control domestic air routes.

One of the leading critics and authorities of air regulation, Dr. William A. Jordan, has declared that air fares in the United States are 40 to 100 percent higher than necessary as a result of C.A.B. reguation. He contends further that such regulation has sharply cut into airline profits by reducing em-

ployee productivity and forcing the airlines to purchase un-
needed equipment.

Dr. Jordan, a professor of managerial economics at York
University in Toronto, has worked for four airlines over a 27
year period. He bases his estimates on comparisons of federally
regulated airlines with intra-state carriers operating within
Texas and California, which do not come under C.A.B. regulation. According to Dr. Jordan, existing fares were 75 to 100
percent higher than they would be without regulation on flights
of medium distance and transcontinental fares were 100 percent higher. Estimates that total savings to all consumers resulting from ending C.A.B.'s regulatory functions would
amount to 3.5 billion dollars.* The Interstate Commerce
Commission's record is comparable. Established in 1887 to
protect consumers and rail lines from pricing and rate wars,
the agency today has more than 2,000 employees and 78
offices across the country. Railroads, interstate trucking and
barge lines are all under the agency's jurisdiction and the essential result of its activities has been to lessen competition.

It should be noted that those who Leonard Read refers to
as "the exception makers" exist in **every** field of endeavor,
however, as the following examples indicate:

"I am for free enterprise but I favor federal aid to education."

"I believe that each person has the right to the fruits
of his own labor but I am for compulsory Social Security."

"I stand foresquare for private property but we need
subsidized navigation in order to obtain cheaper coal
for our steam plants.

"I favor the free-market economy but T.V.A. has my
endorsement."

"I subscribe to the principles of limited government
but it is quite alright for the State to prescribe and
enforce minimum wages and maximum hours of
work."[7]

Last (but by no means the least) contributor to economic ignorance is the media.

Although the media includes television, radio, newspapers, magazines, etc., there is little doubt that the three major televison networks alone wield more influence on public opinion than even the government itself — which uses those major networks to project its information and opinion. Just as the primary and secondary educational system has contributed to our plight, the "adult educational system" controlled by the major networks has made its indelible impact.

For many reasons, which this volume shall not delve into, the media tends to purvey views which do not include the free-market economy as even a possible solution to the overwhelming supply of apparent or alleged troubles that flow from your television screens. By simply **not covering** or giving time to proponents of less government, such views and information are buried. It would seem, in addition, that those who encourage more intervention and control of our lives receive vast coverage not only in the news but throughout the communications and entertainment world.

By way of a small test: have you heard any of the views or well-documented statistics covered in this volume expressed on any major network during the last two or three years?

*As this book goes into print considerable relaxation of C.A.B. and I.C.C. regulations has resulted in some of the benefits predicted. More deregulation is obviously in order, and the C.A.B. will be terminated in 1983.

Part II

The History And The Principles

"History is a voice forever sounding
across the centuries the laws of right
and wrong. Opinions alter, manners
change, creeds rise and fall, but the
moral law is written on the tablets of
eternity."

James A. Foude

CHAPTER VII

OUR AMERICAN HERITAGE

We have identified and examined the problems. Any search
for solutions requires a look at the all-too-brief history of individual liberty and the principles that shaped it.

Where do we find our most modern example of these principles? In our own Declaration of Independence, Constitution,
and Bill of Rights!

Historically, these principles emanate directly from the Ten
Commandments, the teachings of Christ, and the civil orders
established in Greece and Rome. Using this thread of moral
law, the founders began to weave this cloth of "Men and
Governments." Into its making they incorporated the ideals of
John Calvin and of Martin Luther; of Wyclif, of the King
James Bible, and of the Magna Charta.

From John Locke's *Treatises on Government* came clarification of "endowed rights"; from Sir William Blackstone's
Commentaries flowed the deep perceptions of justice and the
inseparability of human and property rights.

Strengthening these concepts were the experience and

reflections of our Pilgrim fathers with their Mayflower Compact, the Petition of Rights — and blended into these, the realization of Plymouth and Jamestown.

Herein lies the cornerstone of our thesis!

Man cannot separate his spiritual life from his economic or political ideas and remain free, for into a spiritual vacuum flows the loss of personal discipline and invites inevitably the tyranny of regimentation!

Nature abhors a vacuum!

A glance at Governor Bradford's diary recounting the experiences of the Plymouth Bay Colony from its inception in 1620 provides some interesting insight into what might be called pilgrim's progress.

Most of our history books fail to recount that, in the beginning, the pilgrims established a communal economic system; in short, communism in its simplest form. Each was to produce according to his ability and contribute his production to a common storehouse from which each was to withdraw according to his need. Human nature existed then as it does today, and within a short time, the pilgrims found themselves on the edge of starvation.

According to Governor Bradford's account, he and his advisors called the colonists together and suggested that each might do whatever he chose with the results of his labor. I quote from the governor's diary as to the consequences:

"This had very good success; for it made all hands very industrious, so as much more corne was planted than other waise would have bene by means the gov. or any other could use, and saved him a great deall of trouble, and give farr better contente. The women now wente willingly into the field, and tooke their little-ons with them to set corne, which before would aledg weakness, and inabilitie; whom to have compelled would have bene thought tiranie and opression . . . By this time harvest was come, and instead of famine, now God gave them plentie, and the face of things was changed, to the rejoysing of the harts of many, for which they blessed God . . . and some of the abler sort and more industrious had to spare, and sell to others, so as any generall wante or famine hath not been amongest them since to this day."

It might well be said that, at that moment, the uniqueness of what has been referred to as the American spirit was born, and with it, the sparks destined to set off the American revolution about two hundred years later.

And what of the American pioneers who followed? Certainly they were not intellectuals in today's sense, but they understood tyranny and regimentation — and they wanted none of it! Simply, perhaps because there was little or no government in existence, they acknowledged that the source of their great gifts of life, liberty, and property was neither Man nor Government. For the same reason, coupled with an intense love of individual liberty held only by those who have experienced tyranny, they grasped the simple proposition that their personal liberty and freedom of choice rested almost entirely on their willingness to assume personal responsibility and seek its handmaiden, opportunity.

Perhaps the best possible way to describe the attitude of the American pioneer would be to borrow this colorful phrasing of my good friend, Paul Harvey:

In but a few years, free men raised themselves and their society to a pinnacle of progress unapproached in all the ages.

When America's early pioneers first turned their eyes toward the West, they did not demand that somebody take care of them if they got ill or got old. They did not demand maximum pay for no work at all. Come to think of it, they did not demand much of anything — except freedom.

They looked out at those rolling plains stretching away to the tall, green mountains, then lifted their eyes to the blue skies and said, "Thank you, God. I can take it from here."

This nation was not carved out of the wilderness, as some say.

It was scratched and chopped and dug and plowed and hammered and clawed out.

No government in history ever gave its citizens what hardworking Americans with their sleeves rolled up have earned for themselves.

Our citizens stood on their own feet and asked nothing for nothing and elected leaders to match.

There was poverty, but there was opportunity. There were hardships, but there was hope. There was security.

Here, at last, was the security men had sought for six thousand years.

A land in which a man was entitled to all the prerogatives of a man.

He set his own limitations. Nobody else did.

He could climb as high as he could carry his own weight.

Because he got wherever he was under his own steam, he was secure.

Some failed and failed to rise again. So there were poorhouses, as well as mansions. That was the important part. The difference between the nation and the world's older ones being that here the only things which prevent the man in the poorhouse from living in the mansion were his own limitations."[1]

With this freedom and responsibility was born a character known the world over as the American spirit. Based on self-reliance, freedom of choice, the right to own property, and the right to retain the fruits of one's labor, this character built the wealth, the historic virtue, and strength of the United States!

This is the kind of attitude and environment that prevailed during the one hundred and fifty-six years between the beginnings of the Plymouth Colony and the work of Thomas Jefferson and his committee as they proceeded to draft the Declaration of Independence. More than ten years of additional experience was added before the expository debates of the Federalist Papers appeared as prologue to the signing of the Constitution in 1787, and another four years before adoption of the first ten amendments, usually referred to as the Bill of Rights.

The virgin land and the freedom of all to develop it into the biblical "land of milk and honey;" an appreciation of the laws of God and human nature, all coalesced in the founding fathers to produce our unique, and great, basic documents.

(1) The basic premise that separates the American experiment in Man-Government relationships from all others is contained in the second paragraph of the Declaration of Independence:

> We hold these truths to be self-evident, all men are created equal, that they are endowed by their Creator with certain unalienable Rights, that among these are Life, Liberty, and the pursuit of Happiness. That to secure these rights, Governments are instituted among Men, deriving their just powers from the consent of the governed . . .

(2) The conditions surrounding the last sentence of the instrument must be familiar if we are to understand the passion for personal liberty held by the signers.

> And for the support of this Declaration, with a firm reliance on the Protection of Divine Providence, we mutually pledge to each other our Lives, our Fortunes and our Sacred Honor.

It must be remembered that these were men with much to lose, for they were — for the most part — men of means. They stood to gain nothing in terms of money, material, or land — and everything to lose! They were well educated. Twenty-four were lawyers and judges. Eleven were merchants of one variety or another, and nine were farmers and plantation owners. They were willing to trade their security and well-being for the struggles of an embryonic nation at best, or a hangman's rope at worst!

Almost to a man, they paid a heavy price! Nine were reduced to poverty within a very short time. Five were captured by the British, imprisoned, and died within a few years. Twelve had their homes, farms, or plantations sacked, looted, burned by the British. Nine died during the war, either from bullets or personal hardship. Few survived to live out natural lives.

They pledged — and they paid — and, in doing so, they gave birth to your freedom![3]

The Constitution (and the Federalist Papers debating its provisions) and the Bill of Rights consistently ground themselves on the principles developed in these chapters.

The founding fathers illustrate clearly their recognition of the absolute need of individual liberty. The documents shine with their understanding of both the imperfection of man as well as the tendency toward power and tyranny inherent in the nature of government.

The founders attempted to establish a limited government designed not to govern, but rather to referee. The concept is much like that of a football game. There are referees on the field whose job it is to interpret the rules of the game. They do not attempt to change the rules in the middle of the game. For if they did, utter chaos on the field would be the inevitable result!

The need for adherence to principle is well stated in the Constitution of Vermont, the fourteenth state admitted to the Union! "... that frequent recurrence to fundamental principles and a firm adherence to justice, moderation, temperance, industry, and frugality are absolutely necessary to serve the blessings of liberty and keep government free."

It is not my purpose to attempt a thorough analysis of the Federalist Papers, the Constitution, or the Bill of Rights. I would be remiss, however, if I didn't take a close look at a few key areas of these instruments which directly reflect the probable thinking of the founding fathers — and which reflect the premises involved in the principles they endorsed.

Did the founding fathers endorse the absolute need for individual freedom and creativity? Did they recognize the imperfection of all men and the danger of allowing government to extend its power too far? Did they see the fallacies of a "pure majority" concept? Did they realize the immorality in allowing some men to rule other men? Did they see the need for an environment that would encourage responsibility and hold men accountable for their actions? Did they understand that government creates no wealth?

Let us take a look.

It should be emphasized that it is not my intention to establish, or even suggest, that these documents are perfect, for the success or failure of any formula pertaining to Man-Government relationships depends upon the adherence to the principles involved in its birth over the generations that follow. A document or contract of any nature is only effective if its principles represent a consensus of idea and opinion.

The preamble proceeds to set the tone!

"We the people of the United States, in order to form a more perfect union, establish justice, ensure domestic tranquillity, provide for the common defense, promote the general welfare, and secure the blessings of liberty to ourselves and our posterity, do ordain and establish this Constitution for the United States of America."

To *ensure domestic tranquillity, provide for the common defense* — these meet our moral test by protecting our endowed rights from one another and from outside usurpation; leaving us free as individuals to exercise our God-given talents in creativity and work by turning the protection function over to government. *To establish justice* — a system of courts meets our test. They serve as an objective third party to decide when I infringed upon your rights and you on mine. This is the beginning of government by law rather than by men and a recognition of the imperfect nature of all men. *To promote the general welfare* is a clause to which we will give considerable attention in later paragraphs.

Article I, Sections 1 through 7, Article II in its entirety, and Article III all deal to a great extent with the division of power between the legislative, executive, and judicial branches; clear testimony to the fear of the founding fathers of unchecked power.

"The power to tax involves the power to destroy."[4] The truth in this statement provides the root of justifiable debate concerning Article I, Section 8 of the Constitution. Known as the taxation clause, it contains two controversial locutions. On these two points, much of our Man-Government relationship hinges in terms of property rights, and therefore, human rights.

It reads (and note the punctuation — for whether the American people realize it or not, it might rightly be referred to as the biggest semi-colon in the world): "The Congress shall have the power to lay and collect taxes, duties, imposts and excises, to pay the debts and provide for the common defense and general welfare of the United States; . . ."

Section 8 then proceeds to list seventeen specific purposes for which the Congress shall be allowed to tax.

Of particular interest to us is the fact that, since the early 1930's, the tendency has been to interpret both "Promote the general welfare" as stated in the preamble and "general welfare" as phrased in Article I, Section 8 as carte blanche authorization to tax for any purpose whatsoever! The punctuation alone should serve as clarification of intention, for it is most obviously a general phrase followed by a semi-colon and, in turn, followed by the specifics covered by the generality.

If this isn't adequate, there can be little doubt as to intention if we but read James Madison's comments in *Federalist Paper 41,* and again in *45.* In replying to objections to the phrase as written, he stated:

"But what color can the objection have, when a specification of the objects alluded to by theses general terms immediately follows, and is not even separated by a longer pause than a semi-colon? If the different parts of the same instrument ought to be so expounded, as to give meaning to every part which will bear it, shall one part of the same sentence be excluded altogether from a share in the meaning; and shall the more doubtful and indefinite terms be retained in their full extent, and the clear and precise expressions be denied any significa-tion whatsoever? For what purpose could the enumeration of particular powers be inserted, if these and all others were meant to be included in the preceding general power? Nothing is more natural or common than first to use a general phrase, and then to explain and qualify it by a recital of particulars."

Again, in his *Federalist Paper 45,* James Madison contin-ued:

"The powers delegated by the proposed Constitution to the Federal Government are few and defined. Those which are to remain to the state governments are numerous and indefinite. The former will be exercised on external objects, as war, peace, negotiations and foreign commerce; with which last the power of taxation will, for the most part, be connected. The powers reserved to the several states will extend to all the objects which, in the ordinary course of affairs, concern the lives, liberties and properties of the people, and the internal order, improvement and prosperity of the state."

As to the phrase, "promote the general welfare" as used in the preamble, both our principles, as well as the entire tone and attitude of the Constitution, would support the conclusion that the founding fathers intended that the purpose could best be served by protecting individuals from violence against their persons and property so that they might promote their own general welfare without interference. Most certainly, they did not intend the clause as an open-end authorization to Congress to redistribute the fruits of people's labor for any and all purposes for which it might see fit!

The Constitution is, more than anything else, a series of prohibitions against the power of federal government. The Bill of Rights provides additional support for this contention, in particular in the ninth and tenth amendments.

Amendment IX. "The enumeration in the Constitution shall not be construed to deny or disparage others retained by the people."

Amendment X. "The powers not delegated to the United States by the Constitution, nor prohibited by it to the states, are reserved to the states respectively, or to the people."

There is little question that the Declaration of Independence, the Constitution, and the Bill of Rights are the written embodiment of some premises and philosophical principles agreed upon by the framers of those documents.

"Nothing is so easy to deceive as one's self; for what we wish, that we readily believe."

Demosthenes

CHAPTER VIII

A SUPPLEMENTARY MEASUREMENT

We have directed our attention to the importance of *ideas,* the absolute need of applying a sound method of their measurement, and the establishment of a set of principles which may be used as criteria in evaluating social ideologies. All of this has been directed to the nature of Man and Government — and pointed toward an ideal relationship between the two.

Although few would deny that the character and morality of Man still leaves a great deal to be desired and most would agree that there has been an incredible quantum leap in the power and size of government, many may still ask: "Is it not true, in spite of the above imperfections, that we never had it so good?"

How does the United States of America measure up to the principles expresses in the Declaration of Independence, the Constitution, and the Bill of Rights? Is our personal liberty really declining?

An evaluation of this sort involves both economic and moral considerations. Reflect on the following:

We have been speaking of documents, and perhaps a significant beginning might be found by reading a few pages in a document which, in the eyes of most, is synonymous with regimentation. I refer to the *Communist Manifesto*, co-authored by Karl Marx and Friedrich Engels in 1848. Specifically, I refer to pages 54, 55 and 56 of the Samuel Moore translation published by Henry Regnery Company in 1954, in which Karl Marx considers the methods by which a free society shall be destroyed as the prologue to the firm establishment of Communism.

We have seen above that the first step in the revolution by the working class is to raise the proletariat to the position of ruling class, to win the battle of democracy.

The proletariat will use its political supremacy to wrest, by degrees, all capital from the bourgeoisie, to centralize all instruments of production in the hands of the State, i.e., of the proletariat organized as the ruling class; and to increase the total of production forces as rapidly as possible.

Of course, in the beginning, this cannot be effected except by means of despotic inroads on the right of property, and on the conditions of bouregeois production, by means of measures, therefore, which appear untenable, but which, in the course of the movement, outstrip themselves, necessitate further inroads upon the old social order, and are unavoidable as a means of entirely revolutionizing the mode of production.

These measures will, of course, be different in different countries.

Nevertheless, in the most advanced countries, the following will be pretty generally applicable;

1. Abolition of property in land and application of all rents of land to public purposes.
2. A heavy progressive or graduated income tax.
3. Abolition of all right of inheritance.
4. Confiscation of the property of all emigrants and rebels.
5. Centralization of credit in the hands of the State, by means of a national bank with State capital and an exclusive monopoly.

6. Centralization of the means of communication and transport in the hands of the State.
7. Extension of factories and instruments of production owned by the State, and bringing into cultivation of waste lands, and the improvement of the soil generally in accordance with a common plan.
8. Equal liability of all to labor. Establishment of industrial armies, especially for agriculture.
9. Combination of agriculture with manufacturing industries; gradual abolition of the distinction between town and country.
10. Free education for all children in public schools. Abolition of children's factory in its present form. Combination of education with industrial production.

What you have just read is nothing more than a blueprint drawn up by the social engineers of Communism. The aims and the methods were established in 1848. They have not changed during the past 130 years.

Shall we draw a few parallels?[1]

Plank 1. Government ownership of land. Government ownership of land has increased by almost geometric proportions during the past fifty years to the point that the federal government now owns more than 42 percent of all land within the boundaries of the United States!

Plank 2. A heavy progressive or graduated income tax. Please note that the Communist Manifesto was written in 1848. We had hardly heard of, much less considered, a graduated or progressive income tax until 1913, when the Sixteenth Amendment was ratified. (A fixed income tax of 1½ or 2 percent was levied during the Civil War, but it was fixed, not graduated.) Consider for a moment the analogy suggested by Leonard Read, president of the Foundation For Economic Education. "Utilizing a forty-hour work week as a basis, the average American works all day Monday and Tuesday for the government before he begins to work for himself. The highly productive or exceptionally creative American works all day Monday, Tuesday, Wednesday and Thursday for the government before he begins to work for himself!"

The income tax payments of the largest corporations in the major industries often run to two or three times the amount paid to the owners (stockholders)!

Here is another simple analogy to illustrate the effects of this kind of re-distribution.

Suppose for a moment that you are a student who has studied extremely hard for an examination and received a grade of 90. Now let us assume that another student received a grade of 50. Now consider seriously just what your reaction would be if your instructor advised that he was going to take 20 points from your grade and give them to the other students so that you would each have a grade of 70. Ask yourself: just how hard would you study for the next examination? Obviously, not very hard, because you will not receive the fruits of your labor. And, how hard do you suppose the student who received the original 50 is going to study? The answer is again most obvious. Why should he? After all, he will receive the results of your labors in any case. Frederick R. Kappell of American Telephone and Telegraph put it succinctly in his book, *Vitality In A Business Enterprise*, when he suggested that the old adage, "Nothing ventured; nothing gained" becomes even more truthful when it is reversed to, "Nothing gained; nothing ventured."[2]

In this simple observation of human nature we find a fundamental truth as to why all collectivist experiments have eventually failed. If the significant fact that governments produce nothing is brought to mind, it becomes clear that under any plan involving large amounts of redistribution from those who work and create to those who do not, or cannot, results in less and less production. Finally, the point is reached when there is so little produced in total that even those who had little in the beginning will have even less. *Even a government cannot redistribute that which hasn't been produced.*

It is true that the pump may be primed temporarily with government deficit spending. Such measures result eventually in severe inflation and the medium of exchange becomes almost worthless in terms of buying power.

Plank 3. Abolition of all right of inheritance. The most expedient method of accomplishing this objective would be with a device known as "inheritance tax." What better way (to quote Marx) to "wrest, by degrees, all capital from the bourgeois?" A man in the United States today may have his estate taxed at a rate as high as 77 percent!

Plank 5. Centralization of credit in the hands of the State, by means of a national bank . . ." The Executive Branch as well as Congress seek to exercise control over the independent Federal Reserve System in various ways. Government control of credit through interest rates can only be classified as "centralization of credit."

Plank 6. Centralization of the means of communication and transportation in the hands of the state. The Federal Communications Commission, the Interstate Commerce Commission and the Civil Aeronautics Board in essence control transport and communications even though government is not the owner.*

Plank 7. Extension of factories and instruments of production owned by the state. The government owns far more enterprises than people realize, including the massive post office, which required heavy subsidies (unlike private package carriers, which earn profits).

Let us take a look at just a few of hundreds of business enterprises operated by the Federal Government in direct competition with privately operated enterprises. These businesses operate without apparent constitutional sanction and pay no taxes as their privately operated competitors must. In spite of their built-in tax advantage, these businesses averaged losses of 19 billion dollars per year between 1959 and 1965. In order to cover these losses, you paid $94,295,643,410. in taxes during that period. (Although I haven't researched recent results, I suspect they're even worse.)[3]

Item: ABACA Production and Sales Program. This Government venture into the manufacture of Manila hemp cost the American taxpayers more than $28,856,086. over a 14-year period.[4]

Item: Alaska Railroad. This venture operated not only a railroad with a bizarre engineerng oddity, a steam-heated tunnel (which has never functioned properly), but also river boats, hotels, saloons, restaurants, commissaries, mess halls and dormitories. This enterprise had cost you, the taxpayer, $59,786,081. up to June 30, 1954.[5]

Item: Eskimo Dwellings Corporation. This activity was launched with the avowed purpose of stimulating construction of Eskimo housing in "remote areas." At the time of the 1958 Budget Report, this little effort had cost you, the taxpayer, $1,580,000.[6]

Item: Rama Road, Nicaragua. The Bureau of Roads of the Department of Commerce (which has no authority outside the boundaries of the United States) partially built this road through the Nicaraguan jungle, where population is sparse, traffic is nonexistent, and automobiles unknown. It has cost you, the American Taxpayer, $12,000,000.[7]

Item: TVA Fertilizer Program involving the construction and operation of two nitrate plants for munitions purposes. They weren't completed until seven years after the war, at which time they were assigned to the production of fertilizer. At this task both plants failed at a cost to the American taxpayer of $125,433,493.[8]

The list continues with hundreds of such examples containing such bizarre names as Central International Office for the Control of Liquor Traffic in Africa, Cuba Nickel Company, Indian Arts and Crafts Fund, International Bureau for the Unification of Penal Law, Leather Shoes and Allied Products Division, etc.

Plank 8. Equal liability of all to labor. Establishment of industrial armies. The size and political power of the major American labor unions yield strong evidence of this trend.

Plank 10. Government ownership of schools. The constant increase in the scope of federal aid to education and the automatic federal control that accompanies it could hardly be more evident.

We have simply engaged in an exercise of comparison to illustrate, to a small degree, that a departure from principle leads directly to the loss of individual liberty!

*Deregulation bills have now been enacted into law which will eliminate the CAB in 1983 and lessen the powers of the ICC to control the trucking and railroad industries.

"Truth is the foundation of all knowledge and the cement of all societies."

John Dryden

CHAPTER IX

THE SEARCH BEGINS

An attempt to measure anything, even ideas, must be based on some standard unit from which to work. In the realm of ideas, we are at once faced with the assumptions or premises — call them what you will — upon which we can generally agree. The search for right principles is an eternal process to be pursued but never achieved in its entirety.

This chapter rests on the wisdom of Marcus Tullius Cicero: "Not to know what has been transacted in former times is to be always a child. If no use is made of the labors of past ages, the world must remain always in the infancy of knowledge."

A look to history, then, is very much in order; and if, like Janus, the Roman God with two faces, we heed the past with one pair of eyes and, upon consideration of Man's experience, scan the future with our second pair of eyes, some initial truths begin to emerge!

Throughout recorded history, mankind has struggled against starvation. The vast majority of the human family has been ill-fed, ill-clothed, and ill-housed; and the condition remains unchanged, even today, in much of the world.

Suddenly, in less than 160 years — just a small speck of time historically — in one small area covering approximately 7 percent of the world's land, 6 percent of the world's population — we found ourselves with more than 50 percent of all the world's products and possessions and with surpluses of foodstuffs! From log cabins to air-conditioned homes, from horseback and ox-carts to automobiles and jet airplanes, the phenomenon is fantastic!

Why and how could the miracle occur? Some questions are definitely in order. Did we have greater natural resources than Europe? Or China? Or South America? The answer is no! Did we have more tools? Again, the answer is no! At the outset of their almost unique adventure, our early pioneers had little more than axes with which to clear the land. Let us take a closer look.

During most of man's history, he has lived under the influence of pagan concepts. Though widely varied in form and belief, literally all pagan teachings contained a thread in common — the doctrine that man was helpless; that he was wholly at the mercy of relentless forces beyond his control. In short, **he was not responsible for either his actions or his future.** I submit that the key to the uniqueness of the American Idea found its birth when Moses reduced the teachings of Abraham to a written code of conduct, a moral law, the Ten Commandments. This was the first recognition of man as a self-controlling individual, responsible for his own thoughts, his own words, and his own actions. The Decalogue recognized that man was a dual entity, spiritual as well as material. Most important of all, however, this code of conduct recognized that from God, the Creator, man has received his greatest and his only rights — the God-given right to property, and not from other men, a government, or state.

Whether or not the reader believes in God, consider the rather obvious proposition that man was here first, prior to a government or a state, and that his very life and existence could not possibly have been a gift of either. Consider further the theorem that his existence then depended upon his right to be free to attempt to sustain his life. This freedom, or right, to maintain and improve his lot is patently an extension of this right to life. It, too, is clearly not a gift of the state. And finally, if we accept "Thou shall not steal" as a valid part of our moral code, the God-given right to hold private property, honestly acquired or inherited, would appear to be unshakable; for without it, you would acquire the contrary right to take my property at will and by force, if necessary, and my disposition toward your property would be similarly aggressive.

The brilliant French political scientist, Frederic Bastiat, stated the proposition with devastating clarity. "Life, liberty and property do not exist because men have made laws. On the contrary, it was the fact that life, liberty and property existed beforehand that caused men to make laws in the first place.[1]

Or we might phrase the premise in another way: In measuring the merit of an idea involving the relationship between Man and Government, the first principle of measurement should be posed with this question:

Does this idea encourage or discourage the utilization of free, creative human energy?

In any case, we can agree that individual freedom is an absolute ingredient in our Man-Government relationship.

Unfortunately, the term freedom has been scrambled to the point that we must define it before we can establish a sound and usable premise. Are freedom and license the same? Is "to covet" compatible with "to aspire"? Is it freedom to? Or freedom from?

Edmund A. Otpiz, a distinguished scholar with the Foundation for Economic Education, put it beautifully when he stated, "Freedom is a complicated subject. How, otherwise, could we account for the fact that man has had so little of it during the checkered history of this planet?"[2]

Just what do we mean when we use the term individual freedom?

"To have freedom is only to have
that which is absolutely necessary to
enable us to be what we ought to be,
and to possess what we ought to possess."

Ibn Rahel

CHAPTER X

FREEDOM TO OR
FREEDOM FROM

The history of human freedom — even the use of the term
itself — is a tangled topic. History is full of Man-Government
relationships; strong governments, one-man rule, government
ownership of the means of production, government control of
the means of production, government guaranteed security, ad
infinitum.

Stalin and Khrushchev constantly referred to the freedom of
the Soviet People's Republic; Hitler based his aggression on
the need for the freedom of the German people; Castro speaks
of freedom of the Cuban people; even Mao Tse-tung, in his
book, *China's New Democracy* (written in 1944), as well as
constantly in his orations, spoke of the freedom of the Chinese
people!

Four thousand years ago, the Code of Hammurabi imposed
a rigid system of controls over wages, prices, production, and
consumption. Personal freedoms as well as economic freedoms
went down the drain — and Babylon followed down the same
drain. The vaunted freedoms of Athens were subjected, during

the fourth century B.C., to regulations and scrutiny of grain inspectors and government agents of all descriptions. The system and the society were eradicated in short order. During the reign of the Roman Emperor Diocletian, a document of almost unlimited price and wage controls, and invasions of personal liberties, known as the Edict of Diocletian, was proclaimed and it served as a most effective catalyst, as the Roman Empire plunged headlong into the threshold of the Dark Ages.

An inquiry into the provisions of the Constitution of the Union of Soviet Socialist Republics usually provides a jolt to those unfamiliar with it, for it "guarantees" to its citizens considerably more "freedom" than does our own constitution. Article 125 guarantees freedom of speech, freedom of the press, freedom of assembly (including the holding of mass meetings), and freedom of street processions and demonstrations. Article 124 guarantees freedom of religion. At this point, the Soviet document is just getting warmed-up on the subject of freedom and rights!

After a good running start, the Soviet Constitution proceeds to guarantee employment and the elimination of economic crises in Article 118; it guarantees the right to rest and leisure as well as the availability and use of sanatoria, rest homes, and clubs in Article 119; free medical service, health resorts, and maintenance during old age in Article 120; the right to education in Article 121; and equal "rights" for women, including state aid to mothers of large families and unwed mothers, in Article 122.[1] A cursory examination would give one the impression that our own Constitution has rather short-changed us; after all, it guarantees none of these things in its inital form, and only a very few of them in the following amendments.

A little closer investigation, however, begins to bathe the entire subject of freedom in the glaring light of truth and our search for our first principle of measurement and our definition begins to clarify!

The constitution of the Union of Soviet Socialist Republics, though seemingly the origin of an unparalleled series of guarantees, rights, and freedoms, has not provided the citizens of the Soviet Union with these blessings of liberty. The document, typical of almost all efforts involving the relationship of Man and Governments throughout history, clearly designates the State as the source of these sundry rights and freedoms. In other words, your freedom is a gift of the State. Obviously, (and this is the crux of the idea) **the power to extend implies the power to remove.** To put it succinctly, freedom by consent!

Is it sound logic to assume that human rights or property rights are a gift of the State — a gift extended by some men to other men? Historical studies show that almost all societies have been conceived on this assumption.

Wherein, then, lies the uniqueness of the American Idea? It most certainly is not the theory of "checks and balances," for the British employed it prior to our experiment. Regular elections of leadership by the people is not original, for the Greeks and others preceded us in this area. Could it be the division of power doctrine? Federal, State, and local government all engaged in the governing process? No, France and others were ahead of us with this notion.

The unprecedented American Idea is this: The source of Man's rights is not a King, a State, or a Government. The source of Man's rights is not even other men, not even a majority of other men. Rather, as our Declaration of Independence puts it, men "... are endowed by their Creator with certain unalienable rights; that among these are life, liberty, and the pursuit of happiness ..." Further, the uniqueness of the American Idea is embodied in the ideal that government is forbidden to infringe or violate these God-given rights!

For full clarity on this idea, I would like to quote freely and at random from the words of Leonard E. Read, President of the Foundation for Economic Education, as expressed in his *Endowed By Their Creator*:

> The full implication of this idea is expressed in these words of the Declaration of Independence, "We hold these truths to be self-evident, that all men are created

equal, that they are endowed by their Creator with certain unalienable rights; that among these are life, liberty, and the pursuit of happiness." This, quite obviously, is a political concept with tremendous spiritual overtones. Indeed, this concept is at once spiritual, political and economic. It is spiritual in proclaiming the Creator as the endower of men's rights and, thus as sovereign. It is political in the sense that such an acknowledgement implicitly denies the State as the endower of men's rights, and thus, the State is not sovereign. And this is an economic concept because it follows from a man's inherent right to life that he has a right to sustain his life, the sustenance of life being nothing more nor less than the fruits of one's own labor.

. . . Unless we believe that man's rights are endowments of our Creator and, therefore, unalienable, we must conclude that the rights to life and liberty derive from some human collective and that they are alienable, being at the disposal of the collective will. There is no third alternative: **we believe in one or we submit to the other.** If the latter, there is no freedom in the social sense; there is despotism.

If we lack this spiritual faith, our rights to life and liberty are placed on the altar of collective caprice and they must suffer whatever fate the political apparatus dictates. The record clearly shows what this fate is. Russia is the most degraded example, but practically every other nation, including our own, drifts in Russia's direction. Among the Russians, we note that freedom of choice has been forcibly lifted from the individual and shifted to the political collective.

. . . There is another feature of the Moscow apparatus about which we should become acutely conscious; its Godlessness. This is no accident. The political collective would undermine its power if it permitted spiritual faith in the Creator as the endower of man's rights.

... As suggested earlier, no governmental apparatus can lord it over a people who conceive of their rights as deriving from their Creator. This conception makes impossible, among those who hold it, any ascendency of government beyond its principled position. It restricts the powers of government to the exercise of such force as any individual is morally warranted in employing. The individual, as a being responsible to this Creator, has a moral right to defend his own life and liberty and property against fraud, violence, misrepresentation, and predation by others. Lacking this right, he could not discharge his responsibility for the proper stewardship of his own life. Government logically can have no powers beyond those which individuals may properly exercise — if the Creator concept be accepted. Man is free to act creatively or productively as he pleases. Here we have the absence of any and all political restraints on creative action, in short, total freedom from governmental interference in this area.

I have used the term "total freedom." It must be understood that this does not and cannot include actions which impair another's freedom. Freedom, except in its psychological sense, is a special term. Socially speaking, freedom has a place in our vocabulary only as it describes a felicitous relationship of man to man. Therefore, freedom is not and cannot be synonymous with unrestrained action. To do as one pleases, if it infringes upon the freedom of another, is not freedom at all — it's tyranny.

There is one other point that needs emphasis: Merely to agree with the concept that men are endowed by their Creator with the rights to life and liberty is not at all adequate ... many people give lip service to this concept without relating it to its practical, political application. If all of its implications are to be brought into sharp focus in our minds, a bit of cob-web clearing is required — for government, in our ideal theory, is automatically excluded from any action beyond securing the rights with which we are endowed by our Creator. Government tampering with or management of any creative activity becomes unthinkable.

Of great significance in this concept of individual liberty is an unclouded distinction between "freedom-to" and "freedom-from." If our basic idea of freedom is sound in premise and consistent in logic, it quickly follows that what Henry Grady Weaver referred to as the "mainspring of human progress" is firmly entrenched in the freedom-to category. Freedom for each individual to utilize and expand his own God-given talents, in short, his Creator-endowed right to Life, Liberty, and the Pursuit of Happiness, is the touchstone of our initial principle to apply to the relationship of state and citizen.

The freedom-from school is rather well represented in Articles 118 through 122 of the Soviet Constitution. The absolute incompatibility of these two concepts will be dealt with in detail later, but a most analogous condition is described by Starr Daily in his private journal entitled *Through Valleys To Victories* in the chapter, "I Shall Not Want."

In general terms, he points out that he possesses freedom from hunger, freedom from nakedness and cold, freedom from unemployment, freedom from a lack of medical care, freedom from fear of insecurity in old age, and freedom from economic crisis. At the time this was written the author was an *inmate working in a prison hospital.* He was laden with freedom-from, but devoid of freedom-to, for freedom-from is the handmaiden of regimentation.

The first step has been accomplished in our search for an initial premise from which to judge the relationship between Man and Government. Our first principle is individual freedom. This kind of freedom, the unique factor that wrought the American miracle, thus provides us with our launching pad from which to proceed.

> "Perfection does not exist; to understand it is the triumph of human intelligence; to expect to possess it is the most dangerous kind of madness."

Alfred De Musset

CHAPTER XI

IMPERFECTION AND POWER

In our search for principles, some rather obvious but generally overlooked, premises become clearer.

As a businessman and engineer, I am daily considering the characteristics of elements being combined to achieve a desired result. In designing a machine tool, a building, or a bridge, the properties of the material (or materials) to be utilized receive first attention. The design or idea is entirely dependent upon the nature of the materials available! There are no skyscrapers built of butter and no boring mills constructed of rubber.

In an attempt to arrive at unassailable premises to be applied to an ideal tension between Man and Government the first order of business would be to consider the nature of each.

Let us recognize man for what he is! This implies, of course, that we must also consider what he is not.

First of all, he is not perfect! His character is flawed; his knowledge is skimpy; his perceptions are often false.

The very nature of these imperfections leads us quickly to the assumption that man is, therefore, generally incapable of recognizing his own limitations. In short, he tends not to realize that he is imperfect.

Secondly, men are not equal! It is a truism that men are

equal in the sight of God; and contingently, that men should be treated equally under the law. Aristotle put it succinctly in his *Politics* when he stated, "The only stable state is the one in which all men are equal before the law." These concepts of equality apply to rights, privileges, and treatment.

I suspect that, although all things under the sun not created by man tend to be treated equally under the laws of the universe, they are not equal in any other sense. Ralph Waldo Emerson put it well when he states, "Nature never rhymes her children nor makes two alike." Trees, snowflakes, rocks, and flowers would be simple examples of this. I doubt, however, that there are two trees, snowflakes, rocks, or flowers that are exactly equal to one another.

As a sage once said, "All men are created equal. The trouble is that some are more equal than others."

Certainly men are not equal in size, shape, talent, aspriation, and ability! Each is a totally individual entity — and most men strive constatntly to achieve even greater inequality. We continually hear reference to the "common man" and yet few classify themselves as within the category. In fact, further evidence of our tendency to avoid this classification for either ourselves or our associates could be readily illustrated in our desire to secure the services of a very uncommon doctor when we are ill, a very uncommon lawyer when we are in legal difficulty, and a very uncommon general when we find ourselves in a military crisis.

It is evident that we have not attempted to evaluate, at the moment, more than a few of the myriad characteristics of man, but the things that concern us here are (1) his fallibility and (2) his dissimilarity, one to another.

A consideration of the nature of government involves simply an examination of its historical relationship to man.

In every society, government has been synonymous with force. The citizens of Assyria, Persia, Egypt, Greece, Rome, as well as Nazi Germany and Soviet Russia, submitted to state power.

In most civilizations, state power has been pervasive, allowing little or no individual liberty. In some societies, the function of government power was defensive in nature. In most cases, the power of government grew beyond its policing or peace-keeping function into oppression. In all situations, government is made up of men and involves the wielding of power by some men over other men.

Thus, a study of the nature of government involves the study of power and its effect on those who control as well as those who are controlled. Power is a heady wine and its history — without exception — is a tragic one. Lord Acton's dictum, "All power tends to corrupt; absolute power corrupts absolutely," would appear to be as immutable as the Law of Gravity.

Power is sometimes usurped and other times delegated, but how it is obtained is of less importance than how it is used. Excessive power is bad — in business, labor, or government. Of the three, however, government has the worst record, for it is the only one backed by armed force.

It is worth noting that neither the imperfect nature of man nor the power of government are particularly dangerous alone. It is the combination which inevitable courts disaster, for the imperfections of man become magnified by acquisition of power.

Unfortunately, intentions have little or nothing to do with the destructive nature and consequences of power. History is full of benevolent dictators. Su Tung-Po, an eleventh century Chinese poet historian, would appear to be almost prophetic with his comment, "Nothing is so dangerous to a Nation's destiny as an opinionated, but misguided, idealist."[1]

If we accept the idea of the imperfectness or fallibility of all men, we might then tend to concede that "someone" should make their decisions for them in order to protect them and others from themselves. Who should that someone be? Government? Is not government made up of fallible men? Were Lyndon Johnson, Theodore Roosevelt, Abraham Lincoln, John F. Kennedy, Herbert Hoover, or Franklin D. Roosevelt devoid of the fallibility which plagues us all?

And does an imperfect lose these weaknesses when elected or appointed to public office? Most certainly he does not.

Power is what makes a dictator. How he obtains office has little to do with it.

Let us then consider further the results of the errors in judgment and transgressions of morality under varying conditions.

If you or I blunder, the effect visits itself upon our families perhaps, but rarely beyond that limited sphere. If a businessman errs, the effect ramifies to include his associates and probably his customers and suppliers. But if a head of government transgresses, his actions or decisions affect an entire nation: and in the case of a leading nation, the effects expand almost as a geometric progression throughout the world!

It becomes readily apparent that the imperfect nature of man, when combined with the power of government, opens a Pandora's box filled with frightening probabilities. Compounding the problem is the fact that we are left with no choice but to combine them in some form or another, no matter how horrendous the potential. Obviously, it is much in order to search for an idea which will minimize the bad effects of the ingredients we're stuck with. This shall be considered in detail in future chapters.

In spite of the character of the Pandora's box we've opened, we have, in the process, come upon two additional yardsticks which may be utilized in our proposed measurement of ideas relating to Man and Government. Simply by recognizing the nature of each, we arrive at the following questions:

Does this idea recognize that all men are imperfect?

Does this idea increase, or decrease, the power of some men over other men?

"Be not deceived; God is not mocked;
for whatsoever a man soweth, that
shall he also reap."

Galatians 6:7

CHAPTER XII

"WHATSOEVER A MAN SOWETH"

It might be appropriate at this point to re-state our thesis in order to prevent the tendency toward "conclusion-jumping." Specifically, we are attempting to arrive at principles or premises which are fundamentally Laws of Nature or Laws of Historical Experience rather than theories. Utilizing immutable principles as our criteria, we will examine the total relationship between Man and Government. We are not yet ready to seize what might appear to be emerging conclusions! We are, at this juncture, still involved in our search for principles of measurement.

We owe to former Supreme Court Justice George Sutherland the following statement: "The individual has three rights, equally sacred from arbitrary interference: the right to his life, the right to his liberty, the right to his property. These three rights are so bound together as to be essentially one right. To give a man his life, but to deny him his liberty, is to take from him all that makes his life worth living. To give him his liberty, but to take from him the property which is the fruit and badge of his liberty, is to still leave him a slave."[1]

Any discussion of Man-Government relationships must include an examination of rights. Human rights, property rights, and civil rights generally command the attention of the academic establishment and the political community.

At the everyday level there seems to be an assumption that anything is a right. Some of us are inclined to believe that we have a "right" to just about everything desirable on God's earth! A right to an education, a right to adequate food, clothing, and housing, a right to an automobile, a television set, an automatic washing machine, a dryer, a job, a right to almost everything of merit and literally nothing of demerit.

I would suggest that perhaps a confusion in terms becomes evident at this point. Reference to our already established principles would seem to indicate that we could justifiably **raise** a question as to whether these things are **rights** or **economic goals.**

Our only endowed rights are the right of life, the right to be free in order to sustain life, and the right to hold private property.

These other things obviously fall into the area of economic goals rather than rights, but unfortunately, are rarely regarded as such today.

Let us bathe this business of rights in the light of what we have so far discovered.

It is generally assumed today that rights fall primarily into two categories — human rights and property rights. Even a feeble attempt at logic reveals the flaw in this assumption. Property itself has no rights in any form save those of the human being who possesses it. The right to own and control property honestly acquired is a basic human right. (By honestly acquired we mean anything obtained by any method other than force, coercion, or fraud.)

Consider, if you will, the sources and nature of property.

Although we hear constantly that this project or that will be accomplished and paid for by government, a rather unpleasant economic fact of life must be faced: governments create no wealth!

Wealth is created by those who invest capital or work; whether they be the stockholders, chairman of the board, the janitor, the lathe operator, the salesman, or the engineer. All a government can do is involve itself in the distribution or re-distribution of what people create!

It is true that government can direct economic activity in terms of hiring or extending contracts to those in the private sector, but those in the private sector create the wealth and the taxpayer (also in the private sector) simply exchanges his goods and services for the wealth created. The government, per se, has in a sense served as a middleman (at considerable additional cost) but has **created** no wealth in terms of either goods or services.

Consider further, then, the few sources available to the individual in his quest for all material things, from food and clothing to country clubs and yachts. There are only two ways:

(1) He can work, earn, create, or inherit his needs — or the exchange for them. (None of these methods require force, coercion, or fraud.)

(2) He can arrange in some fashion or another to take (or steal) them from someone else who has acquired them through the first method. (This method necessitates some form of force or coercion.)

The choices quickly reduce themselves to **create** or **plunder!**

It has been, unfortunately, a fatal tendency common to much of mankind to prefer, if possible, to live at the expense of others. It would seem, then, a logical and moral function of government to protect this most basic of human rights and prevent the plundering.

Reflect, however, on the following example: If I proceed to re-distribute property or income in my neighborhood by force, I am obviously committing an immoral act. If I hire a professional gangster to do the job for me, the violation is still obvious. What would be your judgment as to the morality of the act if I hire the government to do it for me?

Does this action leave me any less guilty?

If "Thou shalt not steal" is a valid commandment, can we

assume that it is meant to apply to some and not to others? To Man but not to Government?

If laws are passed sanctioning such re-distribution by force, do they not then simply constitute legal plunder?[2]

If such actions are approved by a majority, does this make them right? (The majority concept will be covered thoroughly in a later chapter.)

Perhaps we cannot answer all of these questions with conviction as yet, but we may ponder two more criteria that will help us gauge the Man-Government relationship.

Does this idea recognize that government creates no wealth?

Does this idea authorize taking from some what belongs to them, and giving it to others to whom it does not belong?

CHAPTER XIII

GOOD OMELETTE FROM BAD EGGS?

Further consideration of the Man-Government relationship requires additional analysis of the nature of Man. An earlier chapter discussed the imperfection of man and now a little investigation of just how to deal with this fallibility is in order.

Perhaps the best way to approach the problem would be to ask a cook, "Can you make a good omelette out of bad eggs?" While contemplating the probable answer, you might ask yourself another question: "Can you create a utopian or great society out of imperfect people?"

The obvious answers lead immediately to further questions: "How does one improve the quality of the eggs — or the people?" Perhaps a better way to phrase the question would be, "Under what conditions does man behave at the highest level of morality and responsibility?

Let us first examine the environmental factors.

Society is made up of individuals and the actions and attitudes of society are simply a reflection of the actions and attitudes of the individuals comprising it. It would probably not be incorrect to suggest that most of us tend to behave at a higher level when we function as individuals subject to the dictates of our consciences rather than as members of a group.

We, perhaps, assume our highest level of behavior when, as individuals, we find ourselves in the position of having to face directly the consequences of our actions. Therefore, the environment in which man displays the highest level of behavior is an environment which encourages — in fact, demands individual responsibility!

A person can escape responsibility when as a member of a group, he can consciously as well as subconsciously, in plain old-fashioned American, pass the buck! By way of example: I am not about to sing a solo in church, for I would not be willing to take the individual responsibility for foisting my mellifluous tones upon the congregation! On the other hand, when the rest of the congregation sings out in Sunday-morning enthusiam, I join in without hesitation — for the responsibility becomes shared or diluted. We might even hold the rest of the hymn-singers guilty if we don't like the results.

I doubt that many of us would entertain the taking of a human life. Yet we might stand on the fringes of a lynch mob and feel little guilt, for the human behavior pattern permits us to blame the action on the other members of the mob or rationalize our contribution to the murder as something acceptable to the apparent majority.

Here's an even more pertinent example:

Imagine, if you will, that you are a farmer. From your government agency, you have just received a letter advising that you have $1,140 coming for participation in the soil bank program. Suppose, further, that this letter indicates that, rather than the normal method of payment, your government agency has come up with a cost-saving device whereby you are furnished with an enclosed list of individuals from which you are asked to collect your subsidy. This document suggests that you may utilize the services of your local police department to support your claim if you feel it necessary, but that in any case, you are authorized to collect $49.50 from Bill Brown of 436 Maple Street, $62.20 from Henry Smith of 1429 N. Henderson Avenue, $54.00 from John Smith of 123 Main Street, $65.50 from Bob Jones of 2650 South Fourth Avenue, etc.

And now for the question. Would you, or I, or 99 percent

of our farmers even consider such action? Of course not. Why not? Because we would be swiping other people's wealth. We would find ourselves committing an obvious and flagrant violation of a basic and generally accepted moral law. "Thou shalt not steal." And our victims would hold us accountable!

Consider, however, what happens to our moral values and our sense of responsibility when a huge piece of collectivist machinery called government removes the necessity of our facing directly the consequences of our actions and does the collecting for us — **by force.** The rationalization that takes place is almost unbelievable! Apparently a "laundering" takes place and the action seems cleansed of its unsavory nature. Suddenly, this theft of the fruits of men's labor and its redistribution, by force, to another who has had no hand in its creation, is considered not only all right — but even just!

Even if a few persons question the action momentarily their sense of responsibility undergoes "instant decay" with such rationalization as, "It isn't my fault! It's the government's fault — or the fault of the other farmers — or Peter Rabbit — or even sun spots!" But we take the money.

Let's make the point: It's no more right to steal through government redistribution that it is to steal from others directly.

The only manner in which people's morals can be raised in quality is through the establishment of an environment that encourages, rather than discourages, an even higher level of morality and individual responsibility.

Neither a society, nor a group — no, not even a Nation, possesses integrity, wisdom, justice, morality, or a sense of responsibility. These traits can reside only in individuals and the ability to acquire them rests only within individuals.

An ideal concept involving Man and Government must encourage their development. Just what that concept involves will be thoroughly considered in the chapters following, but it is sufficient to state that we now have our sixth principle of measurement in question form.

Does this idea encourage, or discourage, the highest level of morality and responsibility from the individual?

"From the day when the first members of councils placed exterior authority higher than interior, that is to say, recognized the decisions of men united in councils as more important and more sacred than reason and conscience; on that day began lies that caused the loss of millions of human beings and which continue their unhappy work to the present day."

Leo Tolstoy

CHAPTER XIV

THE MAJORITY CONCEPT

Any discussion concerning the environment factors affecting the Man-Government relationship leads directly to consideration of the majority concept.

Consideration of the majority rule immediately involves a long, hard look at the word **democracy.**

Few words have been as tragically misused, poorly applied, ill-defined, or semantically scrambled as the word **democracy!** We are told that we live in a democracy, our children study textbooks entitled *Problem Solving In Our American Democracy*, and that World War I was fought "To make the world safe for democracy." In fact, the term has acquired almost a sacred connotation requiring all who use it to do so in a religious atmosphere accompanied by organ music.

This attitude creates a strange paradox for several reasons:

(1) The word democracy does not appear in any of our

basic documents — The Declaration of Independence, the Constitution, or the Bill of Rights.

(2) Democracy is defined in the 1928 edition of the United States Army Training Manual as follows: "A government of the masses. Authority derived through mass meeting or any other form of 'direct' expression. Results in mobocracy. Attitude toward property is communistic — negating property rights. Attitude toward law is that the will of the majority shall regulate, whether it be based upon deliberation or governed by passion, prejudice, and impulse, without restraint or regard to consequences. Results in demagogism, license, agitation, discontent, anarchy."[1]

The above definition could hardly be considered a description of something desirable! Yet, only eleven years earlier, we committed our entire nation's resources to "Make the world safe for . . . demagogism, license, agitation, discontent, and anarchy."

(3) In 1958, *The Soldier's Guide,* Department of the Army Field Manual, states the following: "Meaning Of Democracy, — Because the United States is a democracy, the majority of the people decide how our government will be organized and run — and that includes the Army, Navy, and Air Force. The people do this by electing representatives, and these men and women then carry out the wishes of the people."[2]

It should be noted that the second definition does not contradict the first, but appears simply to acknowledge that democracy (by the 1928 definition) is now with us.

Why, then, does this almost universal infatuation with democracy exist?

Perhaps the root of this phenomenon can be traced to an

increasing reverence for group or majority opinion — the acceptance of the idea that the will of the majority constitutes a measurement of political right and wrong.

As Samuel Withers puts it in his *Emerson In Suburbia,* "Emerson's voice cried out, 'Nothing is at last sacred but the integrity of your own mind.' and Suburbia's voices would chorus in reply, 'Nothing is at last sacred but the collective will of the people.' "[3]

At the risk of being considered impertinent, I should like to question the majority concept from several points of view.

Christ was crucified by a supposed majority. Socrates was put to death by the majority. Our own founding fathers would, in all probability, have been hanged by the majority if they had failed in their efforts to establish our independence.

Would the majority be right to vote for, and then arrange to enforce a national religion?

The founding fathers rejected the majority concept for other than the election of officials to public office. They were as fearful of tyranny in the form of a majority as they were that of a king! They refuted quickly the "Divine Right" of either.[4]

Even a perfunctory examination of our basic documents leaves little doubt that the fear of tyranny was paramount in the minds of the authors. The carefully constructed mechanisms of prohibition and restriction against the possible encroachment by a majority against the rights of even the smallest minority makes this self-evident.

Their decision to do so would appear to be historically well founded, for the record of every society that has resorted to majority-rule democracy is riddled with legal plunder, caprice, passion, the perversion of morality and reason, and the collapse of economic as well as personal freedom. Professor Alexander Fraser Tytler put it well almost two hundred years ago when he suggested that a democracy cannot exist as a permanent form of government. It can only exist until the voters discover they can vote themselves largess out of the public treasury. From that moment on, the majority always votes for the candidate promising the most benefits from the public treasury with the result that democracy always collapses from a loose fiscal policy, always to be followed by a dictatorship.

As we discussed in Chapter VI, decisions founded on individual conscience, integrity, reason, and principle are, without question, of a higher order than those arrived at by a group or mob. A majority does not possess these qualities. They are the sole property of individuals!

We do not decide medical questions, engineering design, or mathematical equations by majority vote. In order to arrive at a correct answer, principles and laws of nature must be examined. Should we decide moral questions by the caprice of the majority or in terms of our individual moral principle?

Moral decisions cannot be made in the absence of principle. Majorities do not possess principles!

More often than not, men, who as individuals, think and act with reason and integrity not only condone, but even advocate, proposals which they would not consider as individuals when they sit as members of a group, a council, a board, or a committee.

Leonard Read stated it well in his *Conscience Of The Majority* when he suggested that "Majority support does not remove coercion or force; it does tend to remove conscience. Whatever goodness may be manifested in individual action tends to be lost in mass action."[5]

Worship, or even acceptance, of the consequences of the collective mind is not only dangerous, but fatal, to individual liberty.

As a less important, but nevertheless interesting, sidelight, even the statistical aspect of the majority concept as applied to voting for public officials can cause one to reflect.

At the time of the 1960 elections, the population of the United States was approximately 190 million. Of this total, there were roughly 108 million eligible voters (approximately 56 percent). Of this group of eligible voters, about 64 percent voted, which represents 36 percent of the total population. Had the winner received 60 percent of the popular vote, his support was only 38 percent of the electorate and 22 percent of the population; not 60 percent as the news reports would have us believe. Would you consider it "just" for the 22 percent to impose its will on the other 78 percent of the population?

Regardless of either the quality or quantity of the majority rule concept, there are other aspects of far greater consequence.

The idea of "majority rule" would seem to include the idea of rule. It would seem obvious that, under the principles adopted by our founding fathers, the entire concept of rule was rejected in the interest of maintaining individual liberty. It is clear that a tyranny of the majority was feared as no less dangerous a threat than the tyranny of a king. Acceptance in any degree of the rule idea immediately raises three questions. (1) Rule by whom? (2) What shall be the extent of the rule? (3) Rule to do what?[6]

Thomas Jefferson put it most adequately when he stated, "When it comes to questions of power, let no more be heard of the goodness of man, but bind him down from mischief by the chains of the Constitution."

It should again be emphasized that the majority system as applied to the election of public officials, though subject to argument on some grounds, probably claims more in its favor than disfavor, but in no way, shape, or form constitutes a "right to rule."

The will of the majority is no satisfactory measurement of political right and wrong!

Any treatment of the majority concept is incomplete without consideration of the source of government power. This tends to be a difficult area of understanding but, I can assure you, a most vital one if we are to gain complete comprehension of the principles involved in the Man-Government relationship.

When asked about the source of government power in any alleged "free society," almost everyone will agree that there is but one answer. The people. On this point I am sure we will agree. James Madison is credited with an observation on the subject which, at the outset, and without careful analysis, seems rather complicated. In effect he suggested that no government should exercise any more power over an individual than that individual should exercise over any other individual. Let us attempt to analyze this meaning.

It should be readily agreed that I have a God-given right to defend my life and property against you should you attempt to take either. Fortunately, you are the happy possessor of the same right where I am concerned. In additon, we share the right to combine our efforts in order to defend our lives and property against an encroaching outside force. As a matter of fact, these are inherent rights, vested in every human being and shared equally by all human beings whether there is a government in existence or not.

Note, however, that these rights are defensive in nature. I do not have the inherent right to attack you and you do not have the right to employ aggressive force against my life or property.

It would seem logical that, if we all share these defensive rights equally (and in the same relationship, one to the other), we might turn this defensive function over to a third force (government) in order to relieve ourselves of the necessity of carrying guns or weapons to defend our property. In other words, the mere fact that I possess this defensive right where you are concerned, and you possess it where I am concerned, makes it morally correct for us to organize a government as an objective force which can defend us from one another, as well as from outside. We may not agree with the high cost of this defense at times, but we cannot argue effectively that defensive power placed in the hands of government is immoral in any way.

In addition, a system of courts in order to establish justice and arbitrate our disputes is likewise a logical and moral function of government.

If I should construct a thirty foot sign in my back yard which obstructs your sunshine, we find ourselves in need of an objective third party capable of arbitrating our dispute and enforcing the decision. Am I encroaching on your basic freedoms more by blocking your sunshine, or are you infringing more on my rights by forcing me to remove something which I have constructed on my private property? We may not always agree with the judgment of the courts, but without question, their existence is both morally right and necessary.

On the other hand, I do not have the right to force you to join a club. It matters not how fine the character of the club in question might be, I simply do not have the moral right to aggressively force you to do anything. Remember, the only action I can morally employ is defensive in nature. How can I, then, pass on to government the right to force you to join a private association such as a closed union shop?

I am certainly not allowed to take from you a percentage of what you earn each month, even if I promise to return it to you when you reach your sixty-fifth birthday. From a moral point of view, then, how can I possibly pass on to government the power to enact and enforce a mandatory Social Security program?

We could belabor examples by the dozen, but the point should be clear. Our rights in relation to one another are purely defensive and if we, the people, are the source of government power, it becomes an immoral action to empower government to exercise anything other than defensive power over the smallest minority, even the minority at one, an individual.

It should be suggested that at least some of the confusion relating to the term **democracy** may indoubtedly be traced to our wholesome acceptance of the idea in a social sense.

The elimination of titles denoting royalty and the destruction of a caste system as practiced under feudalism we can, and should, embrace on moral grounds without hesitation. To confuse social democracy with political democracy provides a quick road back to regimentation!

In our consideration of the majority concept, our seventh and final principle of measurement in question form reveals itself in this question:

Does this idea propose doing something collectively which the individual cannot do without committing a crime?

"The restless mind of man cannot but press a principle to the real limit of its application, even though centuries should intervene between the premises and the conclusion."

Henry P. Liddon

CHAPTER XV

A REVIEW OF THE PRINCIPLES

Although there are, without question, an almost unlimited number of principled questions which may be applied to a study of the Man-Government relationship, the purposes of this volume are served with the seven which now form a foundation for our continued examination.

The method by which these principles may be utilized and, indeed, the absolute need of doing so shall, I trust, become evident as these chapters unfold.

For now, it is sufficient to list these criteria:

> *I. Does this idea promote, or destroy, individual freedom and creativity?*
> *II. Does this idea recognize that all men are imperfect?*
> *III. Does this idea increase, or decrease, the power of some men over other men?*
> *IV. Does this idea recognize that government creates no wealth?*
> *V. Does this idea authorize taking from some what belongs to them, and giving it to others to whom it does not belong?*

VI. Does this idea encourage, or discourage, the highest level of morality and responsibility from the individual?

VII. Does this idea propose doing something which the individual cannot do without committing a crime?

It would seem that unless we are blind enough to be in favor of the destruction of individual freedom and creativity, stupid enough to assume that men are perfect, unfeeling enough to be in favor of increasing the power of some men over other men, economically ignorant enough to believe that government creates wealth, criminal enough to be in favor of taking what belongs to some and giving it to others, immoral enough to be in favor of ideas that encourage a low level of morality and responsibility from the individual, and larcenous enough to favor the committing of crimes — we might just agree that the seven principles stated are admirably sound and acceptable criteria for the measurement of ideas.

Part III

The Solutions

"One cool judgment is worth a thousand hasty councils."

Woodrow Wilson

CHAPTER XVI

OBSERVATIONS AND COMMENTS

The late Doctor Richard M. Weaver invited our thoughtful consideration with the title of his philosophical contribution, *Ideas Have Consequences.* The recognition of our birth-right of individual liberty is a consequence of ideas, and so is the threat of eradication confronting those liberties.

How well do the ideas that underlie the consequences related in the last several chapters measure up to our principles?

Did those ideas promote, or destroy, individual freedom and creativity?

Did they recognize that all men are imperfect?

Did those ideas increase, or decrease, the power of some men over other men?

Did they recognize that government creates no wealth?

Did those ideas authorize taking from some what belongs to them, and giving it to others to whom it does not belong?

Did they encourage, or discourage, the highest level of morality and responsibility from the individual? Did those ideas propose doing something which the individual could not do without committing a crime?

Bathe our current Man-Government relationship in the
glare of uncompromising principle and a cause and effect relationship becomes obvious. The horrendous effects that you
have been observing are a direct result of either ignorance or
disregard of our principles of measurement!

At this point I should like to emphasize that it is not my
intent to assess blame for the conditions in which we find ourselves. I do not subscribe to the theory that there is a massive
conspiracy afoot dedicated to the destruction of our way of
life. Of course, there are those few whose major purpose in life
is the destruction of a free society as we know it. International
Communism, nurtured in an atmosphere and philosophy devoid of ethics and founded in atheism, is certainly dedicated
to our destruction, but if it were to disappear tomorrow
morning, the only immediate effect we might foresee would be
a substantial reduction in our defense budget. It is a paradox
to note that we spend approximately one hundred billion dollars a year on various areas of defense in order to prevent the
vicious regimentation of Communism from taking possession
of us by force; then we turn around and support legislation
costing roughly two hundred and fifty billion dollars to adopt
programs almost identical in nature to those we are supposedly
protecting ourselves against!

I'm convinced that, whether they be involved in government,
business, the bureaucracy, education, the union movement, or
the media, MOST people are sincere in their dedication and
their efforts to redress apparent wrongs and alleged injustices.
The reason for the bad results? Unsound premises lead to unsound ideas and, in turn, undesirable consequences.

Nor is it my purpose to sell a particular political or Man-
Government philosophy. An exceedingly important part of my
freedom involves the fact that I do not wish to have others
impose their values on me. Therefore, I must prohibit myself
from imposing my values upon others. Rather, it is my purpose
to clarify principles from which you may measure ideas and
arrive at your own conclusions as to their validity.

Leonard Read causes me to echo the opening statement in
his *The Free Market And Its Enemy.*

My premise is that the destiny of man is to emerge
or to evolve toward an advancing potential, and that
individual liberty is essential to such progress.

The history of mankind teaches the immutable lesson that
whenever men have placed their destiny in the man-made political force of all-powerful government in order to attain social
progress, they doom themselves and their posterity to personal
regimentation and economic mediocracy.

I am reminded of the mythical Greek pirate, Procrustes,
who decided that he was the ideal and proper size and that all
men should emulate him. He would place his victims on an
iron bed of the proper length and, if the individual was too
short, he had him stretched to fit. If the subject was too long,
he had him lopped off to the proper length. He, of course, was
the sole judge of what was proper.

It would seem that we have gradually, but inexorably,
adopted a Procrustean theory of living. Paul Harvey put it well
when he suggested that we now apparently function under the
theory that you can make the small man tall by cutting the
legs off the giant! The fallacy of such a concept is apparent
biologically as well as in terms of political theory.

Most of us have experienced the feeling, on occasion, of being simply overwhelmed by the impersonal nature of the world
we live in. Paul Craig Roberts expressed the contrast well with
these comments:

A person born before the turn of the century was
born a private individual. He was born into a world in
which his existence was attested by his mere physical
presence, without documents, forms, permits, licenses,
orders, lists of currency carried in and out, identity
cards, draft cards, ration cards, exit stamps, customs
declarations, questionnaires, tax forms, reports in
multiplicate, social security numbers, or other authen-
tations of his being, birth, nationality, status, beliefs,
creed, right to be, enter, leave, move about, work,
trade, purchase, or dwell.

He was born into a world in which a person could

travel anywhere on the face of the earth, excepting
Russia and Turkey, without need of a passport, visa,
or identity card. He was born into a world of freedom
of movement of people, money, and ideas. A confident
19th century futurologist predicted that the 20th century would find him freer still.

But by the time of the First World War, the world
into which he was born was on its way out. The period
since has been one of the growing autonomy, not of the
individual, but of the State.

The private individual is an extremely recent and
precarious invention. A central question of our century
is whether he is a mere momentary caprice of history.

Just as private individuals do not exist today in the
Soviet Union or in China, they did not exist in ancient
Egypt. Nor were they prevalent in the Europe of the
middle ages. Private individuals were the creation of
the social revolution that created private property.

I do not use the term social revolution lightly as do
academic sociologists who find a social revolution every
time students change their hair styles or sex habits. I
am speaking of a social revolution which comprises the
social, economic, political, and intellectual history of
western civilization from the 12th century through the
present.

The social revolution through which private individuals were created hand-in-hand with the creation
of private property began with the enclosures in the
12th century and attained its greatest flowering in the
19th century. *Prior to the appearance of private
property, private individuals did not exist. There existed only the rulers and the ruled, Lords and Serfs.*[1]

Have we decided that we no longer wish to be responsible
for our own futures? If this be our wish, it is easily fulfilled.
The price? Our freedom of choice as to what our futures will
be.

What you are responsible for, you have authority over.

Government will always fill a vacuum, and if we either allow or create a vacuum in terms of our willingness to accept responsibility, government will fill it — and, in doing so, assume authority over what would have been our areas of decision. Freedom is the opportunity to make decisions, or to choose among possible alternatives. Character is the ability to make morally right decisions. As freedom diminishes, so does character. *Government can not make man good, or happy, or prosperous!* Historically, the consequences of a generation or two of a "government managed" society have proved to be dire indeed. When the "managed economy" collapses, the resiliency and self-reliance of the citizenry has eroded to the point of almost complete helplessness. In 1922, when Italy's collectivist experiment folded, the people, rather than grabbing their own bootstraps, pleaded for a strong leader to solve their disastrous problems. Mussolini was available. Germany's pattern in 1933 was almost identical, and Adolph Hitler was its consequence. The rest is history.

Holders of power in the governmental scheme of things always claim that their actions are for the benefit of the people. This category includes not only the "benevolent despots," but the tyrants of the Hitler and Stalin caliber as well. As pointed out in an earlier chapter, the current approach is a bit more subtle. Paul persuades the government to tax Peter. In doing so, he not only fulfills his desires, but his conscience is clear because his action has become "legal."

Some might suggest that there is an unsolvable contradiction between principle and practicality. I do not agree. The question is, of course, "How do we reapply our principles in today's exceedingly unsusceptible atmosphere?" I can assure you that there are no easy solutions, and certainly no immediate ones. There are, however, directions towards solutions, and these we shall consider in the final chapter.

The task, no matter how momentous, is worth the effort. He put it well who stated, "If there is no contest, there can be no victory."

"When in the course of human
events it becomes necessary for one
people to dissolve the political bonds
which have connected them to
another . . ."

Declaration of Independence
July 4, 1776

CHAPTER XVII

SOLUTIONS AND YOUR
RESPONSIBILITY

To those who value their personal liberty above all else, the
magnitude of our problems is obvious. Having examined
carefully what *ought* to be the relationship between Man and
Government, we can understand how far we have drifted.
Unfortunately, "what will be" creates an even more ominous
specter — the difference between individual liberty and serfdom.

We tend to forget, I'm afraid, that we have had the joyous
privilege of living during the 200-year speck of time in Man's
history during which individuals were allowed to acquire
property in an atmosphere of personal liberty and freedom of
choice. And let us not forget that *we instituted government to
protect this right.*

Perhaps we have accepted, without realizing it, the idea of
freedom by permission of the state in place of freedom as our
inherent right. In doing so, we have unconsciously accepted the
significant, but totally false, premise that the end justifies the

means. In spite of the idealistic overtones appearing to underlie this idea, the concept presents a vicious paradox. I doubt that you would trust a man who told you that he was going to commit an immoral act now so that he could be totally good later on. The means condition the ends — they cannot be separated. *If you commit evil in order to achieve alleged good, the good is already framed in evil.*

The need for an understanding of the principles of liberty and morality in the minds of men clarifies when you ask the question, "If almost everyone believes in good, how can there be so much evil?"

The late Judge Learned Hand put it this way. "What do we mean when we say that first of all we seek liberty? I often wonder whether we do not rest our hopes too much upon Constitutions, upon laws, and upon courts. These are false hopes; believe me these are false hopes. Liberty lies in the hearts of men and women; when it dies there, no constitution, no law, no court can do much to save it." Recent history would indicate that there is a considerable degree of truth in his observation.

A similar, and most astute, observation made in 1840 may be credited to the great French political philosopher, Alexis deTocqueville.

> I think that in no country in the civilized world is less attention paid to philosophy than in the United States. The Americans have no philosophical school of their own; and they care but little for the schools into which Europe is divided, the very names of which are scarcely known to them.
>
> Nevertheless, it is easy to perceive that almost all the inhabitants of the United States conduct their understanding in the same manner and govern it by the same rules; that is to say, that without ever having taken the trouble to define the rules of a philosophical method, they are in possession of one, common to the whole people.[1]

The truth of the first paragraph is apparent whether we

think in terms of 1840 or the present. The second paragraph recounts a condition undoubtedly existing in 1840, but most assuredly **not** a truism today.

In abdicating our responsibilities to government we would do well to again heed the admonition of Dr. Milton Friedman:

> The power to do good is also the power to do harm; those who control the power today may not tomorrow; and, more important, what one man regards as good, another may regard as harm. The great tragedy of the drive to centralization, as of the drive to extend the scope of government in general, is that it is mostly led by men of good will who will be the first to rue its consequences.

It serves us well to remember that intentions, though admirable, have little merit if the consequences are the loss of our individual liberty.

Once again, Dr. Friedman:

> The greater part of the new ventures undertaken by government in the past few decades have failed to achieve their objectives. The United States has continued to progress; its citizens have become better fed, better clothed, better housed, and better transported; class and social distinctions have narrowed; minority groups have become less disadvantaged; popular culture has advanced by leaps and bounds. All this has been the product of the initiative and drive of the individuals cooperating through the free market. Government measures have hampered, not helped, this development. We have been able to afford and surmount these measures only because of the extraordinary fecundity of the market. The invisible hand has been more potent for progress than the visible hand for retrogression.[3]

Our progress has been in spite of the growth of government power and intervention, not because of it.

It is important to note that the above comments are taken from Dr. Friedman's great book, *Capitalism and Freedom,* written over fifteen years ago when government was but one-quarter of its current size!

Few will deny the failures of one command system after another for **20 centuries of experimentation** — moral failures because man was continuously denied his liberty; economic failures because man experienced almost no progress in terms of his standard of living and personal well-being.

Few will deny that the American idea has performed undreamed of miracles in terms of human liberty and economic progress!

In spite of the overwhelming weight of evidence, the paradox of our time is the fact that the apparent majority of those involved in the political arena, academia, and even the business community continue to recommend infinite varieties of additional government intervention and control. It is only slightly less astounding that the American public seems willing to accept the advice!

We have even been blessed with the example of a classic economic collapse on the part of Great Britain. Perhaps we should heed the words of Prime Minister James Callaghan to the Labor Party Conference of September 28th, 1976.

"We used to think that you could just spend your way out of a recession and increase employment by cutting taxes and boosting government spending. I tell you, in all candor, that that option no longer exists, and that insofar as it ever did exist, it only worked by injecting bigger doses of inflation into the economy, followed by higher levels of unemployment as the next step. That is the history of the past twenty years.

Meanwhile, on this side of the Atlantic Ocean, the evidence is even more convincing. *Massive government spending at deficit levels creates inflation, which in turn creates unemployment!* If you question it, simply look at our own experience. Rising unemployment continuously follows on the heels of a rising inflation rate!

Although all of this might tend to be grounds for great discouragement, let me suggest that there is every reason to be optimistic. *The plain truth is that massive government has been tried and found wanting* — and that fact is now recognized by literally everyone, including those previously hypnotized with the dreams spun by bureaucratic rhetoric.

First of all, it is essential to recognize that the journey from where we are today to a Man-Government relationship that meets our principles is a long and arduous trip. Be prepared, above all, for moments of discouragement. There are times when you will feel that your nation and your world is beyond saving. There are the times to recall the heartening words of Albert J. Nock: "There is a Remnant there that you know nothing about. They are obscure, unorganized, inarticulate, each one rugging along as best he can. They need to be encouraged and braced up because, when everything has gone completely to the dogs, they are the ones who will come back and build up a new society; and meanwhile, your preaching will reassure them and keep them hanging on. Your job is to take care of the Remnant, so be off now and set about it.[4]

It should be recognized that the prevailing orthodoxy is regarded by some, particularly in the academic and political area, as a national dogma. In their eyes, any serious disagreement is considered as deviation bordering on lunacy. Their condescending attitude can be most irritating. Though the realization may be difficult at times, it is important to remember that most of these are good, well-intentioned people. If you question their ideas with our principles, the results can be provocative and stimulating. To attack them as if their ideas or actions were responsible for our plight is worthless, and will make them defensive. Ralph Waldo Emerson expressed several thoughts which fit the situation well.

"For non-conformity, the world whips you with its displeasure . . ."

"What I must do is all that concerns me, not what people think . . ."

"Do your work and you shall reinforce yourself . . ."

"Trust thyself."[5]

Thomas Jefferson defended your position well when he observed, "It is error alone which needs the support of government. Truth can stand by itself." It must also be recognized that it is naive to suppose that the solutions to our problems lie entirely, or even primarily, in the political realm.

It will take time and effort to even locate men and women willing to represent us that are capable of adhering to our values and principles. Of course, politics is important but of little relevance when both candidates for any particular office share relatively the same views and those views do not include at least an attempt at adherence to our principles.

The 1976 presidential election is an excellent example of the frustration of the American voter with the current functioning of the political processs. Approximately 27.5 percent of the eligible voters supported Governor Carter, 26 percent supported President Ford and a predominant 46.5 percent reflected their feelings by staying home!

Although most people regard political action as the final answer to our problems (and who would deny the importance of elected officials of quality and integrity?), I'm convinced that **we,** in fact, **do** provide the key. The following chart will illustrate the concept.

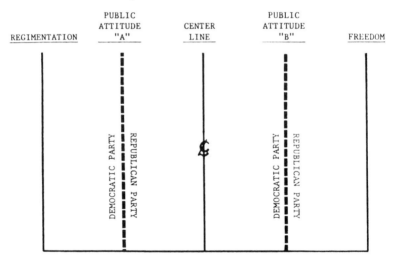

POLITICAL SPECTRUM

If we regard the far left of the political spectrum as *Regimented,* i.e., Communist or Fascist (although normally one regards these as opposites on the spectrum, both obviously represent regimentation and should be cast into the same bag) and the far right as *Free,* i.e., *Free Market* with the resulting personal freedom, we are then able to establish a center-line. If dotted line "A" (left of center) represents what the political establishment thinks is the position of public opinion (it may or may not be an accurate assessment), historical evidence demonstrates that the two major political parties will embrace those centrist views. The result is choices of insignificant difference, both tentatively dedicated to "regimentation by degree." In short, two unacceptable alternatives or no alternative. Conversely, if the political perception of public attitudes arrives at dotted line "B," the same scenario repeats and we find ourselves with choices relatively commited to a free economy, both acceptable to those who favor personal liberty.

Although the above theorem may not describe the normally understood political workings of the system, I'm convinced that it represents reality.

My conclusions? Political realities being what they are, a tremendous effort is essential to educate the public in the principles of liberty.

What, then, are the solutions? There are many sensible and workable plans that seek to reduce the size, cost, and intervention of government, eliminate deficit spending, solve the Social Security dilemma, etc. I shall deal with a few major ones.

Of all the problems we face, the most serious in terms of its immediacy is *inflation!* The primary reason for urgency is the fact that, if we follow the currently recommended remedies and couple them with the possibility of the Federal Reserve Board substantially speeding the rate of monetary growth, we would probably see (1) a sharp, momentary upturn in the economy, followed by (2) a quick reduction in unemployment, followed by (3) double-digit inflation, followed by (4) wage and price controls, and (5) the economic debacle that would most certainly result, with serious recession or depression and great loss of employment.

The most direct route to slowing down this calamitous

tendency is the formulation, promotion and support of *tax limitation legislation at both federal and state levels!* The massive efforts to defeat this kind of legislation, in those few states where it has been attempted, make it obvious that this is the "wooden stake to the vampire's heart" — for all those who feast at the public trough have fought this legislation with fanatic zeal, accompanied by tremendous sums of money.

In its simplest form, tax-limitation legislation simply puts a ceiling on the dollars that a given governmental body (State or Federal) can spend by putting a maximum limit on its budget: a fixed percentage of the previous year's personal income. The previous year's personal income, on either a state or national basis, is a readily available statistic and the percentage utilized is usually based on the year the legislation is passed. (Obviously, there are emergency provisions in such legislation to provide for extreme situations such as geological disasters, etc.) There is simply no disinterested basis for opposition to this form of legislation, for it does not reduce government expenditures, it simply puts a direct brake on the run-away increases and fluctuates with the income of those who pay all the bills! The net result is that the Congress and the State legislatures (or Assemblies) may argue all they wish as to *how* to spend the funds available, but they cannot raid the public till with impunity, as is now the case.

The required companion piece to this is a Constitutional Amendment at the federal level that simply prohibits deficit spending! (This is not required at the State level as the States do not print the currency.) In short, the government is prevented by law from spending more than it takes in, thus a balanced budget!

The combined effects of these two pieces of legislation put an effective lid on taxes and, of even greater significance, prevent the dilution in the value of your earnings by controlling or eliminating inflation, the prime contributor to run-away prices.

A secondary or specific action that might be recommended involves unemployment. Unfortunately, the facts regarding unemployment have been so grossly distorted that they require clarification prior to seeking out remedies. The following facts need to be publicized:

(1) During the ten years ended 1980, the population has increased approximately 9 percent while employment has increased 21 percent. An amazing testimony to the vitality of a free-market system, even under duress.

(2) Based on total population, only 2 percent more people are "not working" today than ten years ago.

(3) There are, rarely, more unemployed people than unfilled jobs in the United States.

(4) Transfer payments (unemployment benefits, welfare payments, and food stamps, etc.) have increased over the last ten years by 223% to over 310.8 billion dollars. (This during the same period that the population grew by 9 percent and the number of working people grew by 21 percent.)

(5) As a result of the above, the Department of Labor estimates that at least one out of every five people receiving unemployment benefits *chooses* to stay unemployed.

(6) The greatest, and constantly rising, area of unemployment is amongst the young and minority groups.

(7) Almost half of the Nation's 7.5 million unemployed were *not* laid off or fired.

Any solutions to the above require a three-pronged approach. (1) The elimination of those things that encourage people to become voluntarily unemployed and stay that way; (2) the elimination of legislation that tends to close down the job-market for the young and minority groups; and (3) most important of all, legislation that encourages capital formation, investment, and the hiring of new employees by the private sector.

The answer to the first of these problems is to severly tighten up in those transfer payment areas that encourage people not to seek employment. Able-bodied unemployed should be required to accept available jobs after a short period of unemployment. This concept includes welfare recipients as well as those on unemployment compensation. To be allowed to live for month after month on the earnings of others when there are jobs available is unthinkable, but it has almost become a way of life with growing segments of the population.

The antidote for the second problem is the elimination of all minimum wage laws, which, though not intending to do so, conspire to hold the youth and minority market off the job rolls. Every time that Congress has increased the minimum wage levels, the percentage of young and minority groups ending up on the unemployment rolls has jumped drastically. The statistics on the subject are incontrovertible.

Black and white teenagers alike could and would find work at $2.00 per hour, but are being prohibited by law from doing so. The white teenage unemployment rate climbed from 10.2 percent in 1948 to 15.3 percent in 1980; and black teenage unemployment, lower than the rates for white teenagers until 1955, climbed from 9.4 percent in 1948 to 37.7 percent in 1980. It has been suggested that, were the government to set the minimum wage at say $5.00 per hour it would succeed in unemploying nearly 100 percent of black teenagers.

The energy crisis, of course, has become an integal part of the overall economic dilemma we must deal with. Certainly, our major objective must be to reduce our dependency on imported oil. Several questions and comments set the stage for solutions.

Do we prefer to support the OPEC economies at the expense of our own?

Doesn't it make sense to pay the American oil companies the profits we now pay OPEC, and in doing so, expand dramatically our exploration and our reserves and reduce our dependence on foreign resources? It can be done.

Does it make any sense to saddle the American taxpayer with the costs to run a Department of Energy that is more than half the total income of the eight largest oil companies during 1979?

The extremely serious side of the energy crisis might be illustrated in the following possible scenario.

The Soviet Union could put a stop to every drop of oil being shipped to the United States and Western Europe. With several major Soviet naval bases on the west coast of Africa and probably control of the entrances to the Arabian gulf, the Soviet fleet would face a United States Navy of approximately 1939 vintage literally incapable of breaking a blockade. Within a matter of less than six months after such action, we might well sustain unemployment levels of as high as 30 to 35 percent in this country due to our inability to run our industrial plants. The consequences would be catastrophic!

In response to this potential crisis we have diddled around at government levels since 1973 and accomplished exactly nothing other than to continue to encourage a dependence on foreign oil and discourage the exploration of new energy sources by the United States.

According to the Energy Research and Development Administration, if we were to allow the price on natural gas to rise to somewhere between $2.25 and $3.00 per thousand cubic feet, we would be able to tap enough gas to last between one thousand and twenty-five hundred years at current consumption.

The solutions are difficult, but obvious.

(1) Deregulation of all energy pricing.

(2) Eliminate the windfall profits tax in total.

(3) Immediately free up nuclear plant construction which is, without question, currently the safest source for key energy requirements and most available over the short term (through the year 2000).

(4) Reduce restrictions on coal usage and immediately go full tilt on coal production and the necessary transportation requirements thus associated.

(5) Dismantle the Department of Energy as quickly as possible, thus eliminating the 8 billion dollar drain on the taxpayers' pocketbook that hasn't produced one drop of oil or one cubic foot of natural gas.

The problem is solvable. We have simply done nothing constructive with this major crisis during the past seven years. The problem of capital formation is, by far, the most important of the three and its solution requires an understanding of who really owns American business, as well as the sources of capital and jobs. The following facts are worth noting:

(1) Contrary to popular opinion, it is not the wealthy tycoons or the "rich" that constitute the bulk of corporate ownership. There are already over 30 million stockholders in the United States and the controlling stock interests in almost all major corporations is constantly passing to an ever-increasing group of new owners. Who are they? The workers themselves, through their pension fund programs. According to the economist Peter Drucker, pension funds now control about one-third of all equity capital and will control half by 1985. The point is that those most damaged by the corporate income tax are not the wealthy, but older and retired Americans receiving pensions, as well as those now participating in pension and profit sharing programs.

(2) Corporate income taxes now contribute only 14 percent of government's income.

(3) As indicated earlier in this volume, the major sources of capital that provide the tools that increase the productivity and, therefore, the earnings of American workers are corporate profits and private savings. The current double tax on dividends, coupled with the tax on personal savings, drastically reduces the incentive to invest.

My recommendation would be the abolition of the corporate income tax as well as the elimination of the income tax on both dividends and savings-account interest. This would stimulate investment in corporate stocks and savings simultaneously and create the capital and dynamic expansion that would solve whatever unemployment problem exists in reasonably short order. At the same time, it would increase government revenues. Frankly, my only reservation on this is the fact that we might very well find ourselves short of available employees to fill the rapidly expanding job market. At the very least, we should eliminate the double taxation on dividends and reduce corporate taxes drastically.

Why not consider the abolition (or drastic reduction) of personal income taxes and in their place, a two-tier national sales tax?

(1) It would be an extremely broad-based source.

(2) It would be voluntary in that it would be part of the price of all consumer products and allow a value judgement.

(3) The lower tier would be applied to all basic products such as food, clothing and shelter. A much higher level would be levied on luxury items to be defined.

(4) It would eliminate an extremely complex and administratively expensive income tax system. (Imagine the elimination of all those IRS agents.)

(5) It would remove the penalties against hard work and success and increase personal motivation.

(6) It would tend to increase savings and investment, thus creating capital and jobs.

In the area of taxes, beyond corporate income taxes and those levies on the interest derived from private savings, additional changes are essential.

It is important to recognize that economic growth must be given first priority, not because it is more important than other goals, but without increased productivity and growth, progress can only be achieved by one at another's expense. In a growth economy everyone benefits from everyone elses success.

Government cannot tax activities that do not take place nor can they distribute goods that have not been produced. The solutions are, again, self-evident.

(1) The elimination or severe reduction of long-term

capital gains taxes in order to encourage investment.

(2) Major cutbacks in personal taxes to increase savings and spending by individuals rather than transferring that choice to Washington, D.C. for ever-increasing, ill-conceived waste. (This will not increase inflationary tendencies when accompanied by tax limitation and budget balancing legislation.)

All of the above would contribute directly and indirectly to increased productivity which is key in terms of reducing inflation.

Another area that requires attention is the Social Security program. It is now costing the average family more than Federal taxes and it is still unable to fund itself!

For purposes of fresh thinking, consider the following:

All funds to be deposited (employer and employee) into any Federal or State approved bank or savings and loan at, for example, 5 percent interest compounded monthly. At year end, the depository of the funds issues a verification slip (similar to a W-2 form) to be attached to IRS tax return. If proper amounts have not been deposited, the corrections would be added to the tax liability.

The beneficial results would be monumental!

(1) Even at a rate as low as 5% and assuming no inflation, a new entry into the system today would accumulate over $300,000.00 in principal funds over his (or her) working life and be able to draw out more than four times the amount the current program provides, **even if the principal was left untouched!**

(2) All those funds flowing into the private sector would be available for new businesses, expansion of existing businesses, productive machine tools, etc., thus providing untold numbers of new jobs. The problems of capital and unemployment would be well on the way to solution.

Of course, there are arguments against such a proposal. Of course, there are an infinite number of details to be worked out. Nonetheless, it is criminal to mislead hard-working Americans as to the efficacy of the current plan, and fresh thinking of this sort is essential.

In terms of creative thinking, consider some of the following:

A change in Article II, Section 1 of the Constitution that would restrict the Presidency and the Vice Presidency to a single six year term of office, plus changes in Article I, Sections 2 & 3, that would limit tenure in the House of Representatives and Senate to a maximum of 12 years. (Six 2-year terms in the House and two 6-year terms in the Senate).

Such alterations would not only tend to eliminate political considerations and contribute to what ought to be statesmen-like decisions, but would reduce the tendency towards life-long careers as elected officials.

Why not make membership to the House of Representatives and the Senate more attractive financially in order to draw the highest possible level of quality, but simultaneously provide incentive for reducing the expense of the tax-payer?

Although Article I, Section 7 of the Constitution decrees that all revenue raising shall originate in the House, the Senate makes its contributions to the tax-payers' burden through proposing or concurring with amendments. If members of both House and Senate were put on a compensation plan that would provide them with their current salaries plus an incentive commission that could raise their personal incomes to over $150,000.00 per year, based on performance involving how many billions of dollars they successfully **cut** from the budget, both of the above benefits would be realized. The environment in Washington today encourages public officials to spend more, rather than less, of the tax-payers hard earned dollars.

The only reason that the above suggestions seem drastic is that we are so accustomed to seeing such decisions made on a political rather than on an economic basis. **From the point of view of solving the problem,** all of the above recommendations would be extremely effective.

The problems have been delineated before, however. Solutions have been proposed from all quarters, seemingly to no avail. The ultimate question, constantly raised but almost never faced; "What can **I** do about it"? Whether you are a businessman, scholar, lawyer, doctor, engineer, teacher, student, housewife, et al, the remainder of this book deals with answering that question as specifically as possible.

"Oh say can you see by the dawn's
early light what so proudly we hailed
at the twilight's last gleaming?"

Francis Scott Key

CHAPTER XVIII

THE POWER OF YOU

Ideas **do** have consequences, and the general solutions suggested within these pages (as well as hundreds of additional concepts of merit) would set a course towards preservation and revitalization for this great Republic that would create a shining beacon of example for the rest of the world.

Almost all Americans are not only conscious of our apparent inability to solve the burgeoning problems we face, but are frustrated to the point of despair by the fact that every effort extended by our government seems to increase rather than lessen the dilemma.

Only a few of our citizens do not endorse the principles upon which this Republic was founded, and even fewer would not favor greater freedom of choice, a higher level of economic prosperity and stability, and an improved feeling of national security in terms of both domestic tranquility and world peace.

If there is any credence to the value of heredity, almost all Americans are descendents of men and women who sought liberty and opportunity at great personal risk in this brave, new world. It demanded courage and decisiveness of character which we, their progeny, most certainly must have inherited. The time to bring those qualities forth is now!

Though general in nature, the first and most difficult step will be the arduous process of reaffirming the informal codes of conduct that governed the behavior of all but a few of our citizens from the early days of our Republic. At the risk of repeating: integrity, lawfulness, professional ethics, loyalty, manners, sportsmanship, and all the rest must again become a way of life. The free enterprise system requires a high degree of self-discipline and self-reliant conduct and, when such responsibilities decline, the heavy handed incursion of government is the price that must be paid. The simple refusal to accept anything one has not earned is an excellent place to start.

How do we accomplish the task? First by setting a personal example for everyone we come in contact with. Second, by an insistence on our part that our business and professional associates adhere to these norms. Why doesn't the legal profession purge its ranks of dishonorable members who discard its ethics in order to line their pockets? Why doesn't the medical profession have the courage to do likewise? Why doesn't the business community take a tough stand within its own house and re-establish a respect for standards of conduct?

It should be emphasized that in all of these professional areas the percentage that flaunt these standards is exceedingly small but, unfortunately, with the help of some irresponsible segments of the media, those few become regarded by the public as the norm.

Third, let us rigorously insist on adherence to the standards by our own children, regardless of the peer pressure from those who simply don't bother.

There is no question that the reinstatement of these standards is the price of liberty.

It should be pointed out that the business leader or manager in the United States today has a responsibility ultimately greater than most. It is essential that we stop defending capitalism and begin proclaiming and rejoicing in its virtues. The former board chairman of one of our nation's leading electrical power companies has stated that the primary responsibility of the business leader is to strive to maintain an environment in which his enterprise will prosper for the benefit of its owners (stockholders), the community within which it functions, the

State within whose boundaries it functions, and the Nation as a whole. The finest business enterprise will eventually fail in spite of good internal management if the environment in which it attempts to function becomes so restrictive that decision-making factors are basically removed from its management.

The American businessman would do well to become more, rather than less, involved with his government, *but it is essential that he cease lobbying efforts that will supposedly benefit* **his** *company or* **his** *industry in terms of favors, protection, etc. Every businessman should lobby for those things that favor the free-market economy that will, in the long run, benefit all Americans at all levels: lower tariffs, lower taxes, deregulation.*

For all of us, the primary concern should be self-improvement in terms of advancing our understanding and articulation of the principles and values to which we adhere. This is the single most important, long-range contribution we can make toward the salvation and/or restoration of our economic and personal liberty!

Although the case for the free-market or willing-exchange economy is primarily pleaded on the basis of its economic efficiency and its miracle capabilities in terms of advancing Man's material well being, I'm inclined to agree with Dr. Benjamin Rogge that another factor is even more important:

> My central thesis is the most important part of the case for economic freedom is not its vaunted efficiency as a system for organized resources, not its tremendous success in promoting economic growth, but rather its consistency with certain fundamental moral principles of life itself.
>
> I say, "the most important part of the case" for two reasons. First, the significance I attach to those moral principles would lead me to prefer the free enterprise system even if it were demonstrably **less** efficient than alternative systems, even if it were to produce a **slower** rate of economic growth than systems of central direction and control. Second, the great mass of the people of any country is never going to really under-

stand the purely economic workings of any economic system, be it free enterprise or socialism. Hence, most people are going to judge an economic system by its consistency with their moral principles rather than by its purely scientific operating characteristics. If economic freedom survives in the years ahead, it will be only because the majority of the people accept its basic morality.[6]

Let me pose this question: **If** we had the knowledge, both economic and philosophical, born of twenty years of concentrated study and debate; **if** we had the time, the staff, and the ability to write, articulate and debate the issues; **if** we had **all** of these things and more, how should we use them in terms of meeting this challenge successfully?

We would individually and collectively engage in the following:

1. We would become involved in the formulation of public opinion through participation in television and radio talk shows and public opinion forums of all types, debating the issues and philosophies with academics, politicians, etc. In addition, we would write regular editorial replies and letters to the editors of all major journals and newspapers promoting the free-market philosophy.

2. We would create and involve ourselves in research foundations to provide the information necessary to enlighten elected representatives.

3. We would monitor legislation at all stages at both the State and Federal levels, be it in committee or on the floor, and barrage our representatives with interviews and letters on important issues.

4. We would propose, sponsor, and write legislation involving tax limitation, constitutional amendments requiring budget balancing, as well as an infinite number of other pertinent issues.

5. We would create and support colleges and universities dedicated to advancing the free-market philosophy as well as adult education foundations with

available lecturers and writers for constant public contact.

6. We would lobby actively both at Federal and State levels — **not** for our businesses or our industry, but rather for those things that encourage a free-market environment. We would spring to the defense of all producing segments of our Nation when they are under attack and expect them to do the same when our industry was besieged.

7. We would monitor and create semi-annual vote-records of legislators at both the Federal and State level and would publicize the results. Such efforts readily expose the public servants who campaign in one posture and, once elected, support legislation with an opposite point of view.

8. We would locate, educate, and promote political candidates at all levels who support the free-market position.

We would become skilled at rebutting any irresponsible journalism by those who have limited accountability. Teachers, politicians, columnists, television news analysts and playwrights can disseminate erroneous theory throughout their careers by generating emotional appeals for their causes. The businessman, large or small, goes out of business if he operates on erroneous theory.

The fact is, we are simply not in a position to accomplish most of these tasks because, with very few exceptions, we are not equipped to do so. Why? Because most of these activities are outside our area of expertise. But what do we do now in areas in which we lack the necessary knowledge such as law, computer technology, public relations, taxes, advertising, etc.? We recognize our limitations and contract or hire the knowledge and experience required! **That is precisely what I propose we must do in order to meet our responsibilities toward protecting and encouraging a free-market environment!**

Although there are many organizations and individuals involved in such work, the following have an excellent track record:

1. Foundation For Economic Education,
   Leonard E. Read, President
   Irvington-On-Hudson, New York 10533
   Telephone: (914) 591-7230
   Since 1946 this fine organization has been
   providing monthly publications, seminars, lectures
   and books, all devoted to the principles of individual liberty and the free-market economy.
   Aimed primarily toward the academic level, they
   have been effective in both adult and young adult
   education.
2. Intercollegiate Studies Institute
   Victor Milione, President
   14 South Bryn Mawr
   Bryn Mawr, Pennsylvania 19010
   Telephone: (215) 525-7501
   For over twenty-five years this group has been
   active on college campuses both publishing and
   conducting seminars for college teachers and students. They have been highly successful in undo-
   ing a half-century of contrary efforts by the Intercollegiate Socialist Society. Many of their
   former students are now in key positions, both in
   academic and government circles.
3. The Heritage Foundation
   Edwin J. Feulner, Jr., President
   513 "C" Street, N.E.
   Washington D.C. 20002
   Telephone: (202) 546-4400
   The largest public policy research foundation
   dedicated to the principles of free enterprise, individual freedom and a strong national security.
   Heritage, whose primary market is the politician,
   provides position papers and ammunition for the
   free enterprise position, keyed to pending legislation.
4. The Fisher Institute
   Sherrill E. Edwards, President

6350 LBJ Freeway
Dallas, Texas 75240
Telephone: (214) 233-1041
This organization's primary purpose is to educate
the public so each individual is better able to decide how public policy is to best serve their self-
interest. It publishes non-political, economic
analyses of public policy issues, and reads for the
"non-reading" public by conducting programs
promoting understanding of free-market concepts
in schools and colleges, civic groups, businesses,
associations, and on radio and television.
5. American Conservative Union (and State
   affiliates)
   422 First Street S.E.
   Washington D.C. 20003
   Telephone: (202) 546-6555
   This is probably the single most effective legislative and political action group putting out constant
   voting records and monitoring legislation at all
   levels. Their affiliates have become active at the
   State levels in formulating tax-limitation legislation and their Conservative Victory Fund finances
   political candidates supporting the free-market
   view.
6. Council for a Competitive Economy
   410 First St., S.E.
   Washington, D.C. 20003
   Telephone: (202) 544-3786
   An effective effort dedicated to furthering the development of free-market economics principles as
   integrated disciplines. Congressional testimony
   and editorials are their specialties.
7. Hillsdale College
   George C. Roche, III, President
   Hillsdale, Michigan 49242
   Telephone: (517) 437-7341
   This small midwestern college is probably the

bastion of free-market undergraduate teaching in the United States. Its Center For Constructive Alternatives provides a constant forum for intellectual free-market thinkers from all over the world.

8. The American Enterprise Institute
   William J. Baroody, Jr., President
   1150 17th Street, N.W.
   Washington D.C. 20036
   Telephone: (202) 862-5800
   A research foundation devoted to current efforts on legislative analysis representing the free-enterprise position.

9. American Conservative Union Education and Research Institute
   M. Stanton Evans, Chairman
   Suite 207
   600 Pennsylvania Avenue S.E.
   Washington D.C. 20003
   Telephone: (202) 546-1710
   Primarily concerned with training young journalists and placing them in media and editorial positions. A.C.U. - E.R.I. annually sponsors the National Journalism Center.

10. Ethics and Public Policy Center
    Ernest W. Lefever, President
    1211 Connecticut Avenue N.W.
    Washington, DC 20036
    Telephone: (202) 857-0595
    The thrust of this organization is to clarify and apply traditional Judeo-Christian values in the public-policy arena. It has been accepted as a source of reliable information and responsible comment in the academic, religious, business, and policy communities. Authors are selected who combine empirical analysis with moral reasoning.

I suspect, unfortunately, that most or all of the above organizations are unknown to most of us, but I can assure you that they have been fighting our battles for decades and with ever-improving effectiveness. They know how to express ideas and reach leaders. They have been consistent watchdogs of the public purse, defenders of the free-market system. They have expertise, the know-how, the knowledge, and the dedication to accomplish the task — **if we will give them the personal and financial support needed.**

The leverage is twofold, however, because in addition to their work, the information which you will receive in terms of economic analysis, pending legislation, voting records, critical bills in a proposal stage, etc. serve to educate us all and equip us to improve our own forensic skills. We thus become a part of the solution instead of a part of the problem.

It should be noted that there are many other organizations doing a superb job, and it is not my intention to exclude them. Those included here have a record of accomplishment, while selections outside of this group should be made with prudence.

It is essential that we not overlook the obvious courses in addition to those stated herein. Though obvious, far too few act upon them. By way of example;

(1) Be certain that **all** of your representatives at Federal, State and local levels are aware that you are monitoring their actions and voting records **not** their rhetoric!

(2) Write to them regularly so that they are cognizant of your beliefs and awareness of of their actions.

It is a minimal effort and it is productive.

The introduction to this volume suggested that "the time has come to regenerate an interest in the foundations of a free and ordered society and, thus, broaden our understanding of its basic principles and traditions."

Unfortunately, individual liberty, self-reliance and the key elements of a free-market economy have undergone a half-century of severe erosion and nothing less than a fervent and sustained effort will restore these values.

A major shift in political winds such as took place in November, 1980 will **not** accomplish the task, although the election of an administration apparently devoted to the objectives of limited government and free-market economics is both significant and important (particularly when accompanied by important shifts in the Congress). The very nature of the unpredictable political allegiances historically practiced by the voting public would suggest short lived dedication in our current climate.

The reason for that condition is precisely what this book is all about. With all too few exceptions both political and legislative decisions are based on reasons other than principles involving individual liberty, a free-market economy, or other consistent values, but rather on whim and obvious self interest.

The vital ingredient in the scenario, therefore, is **you** — and for the following reasons.

In general terms government, the media, and the educators are the primary mass communicators. All three have constant access to the receiving sets of the American public. None of the three are producers in a pure economic sense, but rather play the role of distributors of services and ideas as well as public critics (or supporters) of whatever trend happens to be in vogue at the time. These entities are concerned primarily with distribution rather than production and cannot be relied upon to establish their positions based on any given set of principles.

If you and your children and their children are to enjoy the blessings of a free society you must take the responsibility of becoming a catalyst, a thought leader, and a center of influence even in your own home.

In order to fulfill that role it is necessary to become both knowledgeable and articulate in order to promote and defend the values fundamental to a free and ordered society.

The Fisher Institute, though in existence for a short three years, must be credited with spearheading and implementing this basic concept.

It's the process Albert Schweitzer referred to when he said:
"A new public opinion must be created privately and unobtrusively. The existing one is maintained by the press, by propaganda, by organizations, and by financial influences which are at its disposal. The unnatural

way of spreading ideas must be opposed by the natural one, which goes from man to man and relies solely on the truth of thoughts and the hearer's receptiveness for new truth."

I can assure you it is a never ending process but more rewarding and exhilarating than you can ever imagine.

The next step, of course, is to extend to others, with wholehearted enthusiasm, the ideas that will allow them to become both thought leaders and centers of influence. The organizations listed earlier in this chapter will serve as superb sources for your nourishment.

Another area of great importance is the education for freedom of our young people. Try the following dialogue if you are interested in some real excitement. Keep in mind, our children tend to regard government as solver-of-problems and provider-of-progress.

Let us pretend that the calendar has been turned backwards for approximately 100 years — for simplicity's sake, let's suggest that it is the year 1880. We are gathered here with the task of selecting which of five committee responsibilities we will agree to assume.

The first committee's task is to build a network of superhighways and roads to handle whatever transportation requirements we will face a hundred years in the future, namely, 1980. The second committee's task is to develop a postal system that will cope with whatever we might anticipate to be the needs a hundred years from now, again in 1980. The third committee's task is to invent, design and market a box on which one can turn a knob and watch an event taking place in color anywhere in the world. The fourth committee's project is to invent a device that will carry 350 people from coast to coast in approximately four hours. And the fifth committee's challenge is to figure how to transfer a message around the earth in less than two minutes.

There is little doubt that we are going to discard the last three from consideration, for the idea of color television in the year 1880 is completely beyond comprehension: **we have not even conceived of the radio.** As far as a jumbo jet, this too is beyond our imagination, as we have not yet conceived of machines that fly. As for transmitting a message around the earth in less than two minutes, we have just begun to string telegraph lines, and our ability to communicate consists essentially of yelling across an open field, beating on a drum, or sending smoke signals. Why not at least select a committee to do something that might be within the realm of probability? With that we return to task one. After all, the Romans built roads, so there might be a way that we might accomplish that, or we might consider the postal system problem — perhaps by breeding enough ponies to establish the most all-embracing pony express in history.

The point of this exercise is the realization that the three tasks that we have agreed are impossible have been accomplished in a free society by free men working competitively and cooperatively, while the two simplest tasks we have assigned to a centralized government. The results? Most super highways resemble parking lots close to the large cities, and today you can still ship four quarts of oil from the Persian Gulf to New York City at a lower cost than you can send a letter across the street via the U. S. Post Office! Don't tell me that we need government for progress or problem solving.

I can assure you, you will be in for an exciting two hours of discussion. It should be pointed out that this kind of idea and analogy is directly extracted from the dialogue provided by some of the organizations that you and I are going to hire to help us accomplish the task at hand.

Finally, it is more important that we cast off the self-flagellation that has become the order of the day and start being proud of our accomplishment. It is a paradox to note that the most virulent critics of our way of life are themselves quite well-to-do. Perhaps they suffer from guilt feelings. It is absolutely silly to suggest that we can solve the problems of the rest of the world by sleeping on a bed of nails.

People who work hard and productively are entitled to enjoy their rewards without being told they ought to feel guilty. Why should you feel guilty because the United States has achieved most of what all other countries strive for? It is, in fact, quite easy to make all accomplishments sound like original sin.

Those possessed of the martyrdom syndrome will say "isn't

it awful that the United States, with only 5 percent of the world's population, consumes almost 30 percent of its energy?" Your response should be "isn't it incredible that the United States, with only a twentieth of the world's population, not only produces almost a third of the world's goods and services but has become the industrial and agricultural breadbasket of the world and has given more away to the hungry and needy abroad than all other nations put together?" Your point of view is, indeed, part of your freedom of choice.

And, speaking of solutions, can you imagine the beneficial effect of having our educational system at K through 12 level teaching the basic value that, with the exception of needed voluntary charity, no human being is allowed to live his life at the expense of another?

On January 1, 1966, in his State of the Nation television address, the late Senator Everett Dirksen of Illinois said, "We are the legatees of a great, strong land inherited from those who preceded us. We strive to preserve it for those who will follow us."

There is no easy course, and there is no short course, the entire history of mankind represents a continuous struggle for liberty.

Nevertheless, there is but one right course, and it does not represent one of vacillating values. It would be fatuous to argue that conditions have not changed, for our nation has undergone an almost frantic transformation from a primarily agrarian-oriented society to a closely knit centralized urban-industrial one fraught with new problems. Thus it must be realized and acknowledged that applications have also altered in complexity.

Of course, **some** compromises will have to be accepted in terms of our principles. Limiting government to those functions that eliminate fraud, coercion, and force would be correct, but, undoubtedly, not achievable overnight. We must insist, however, that our governmental servants not only become cognizant of the principles — but that they make every effort to apply them.

The principles governing our actions have not changed.

They are being violated on a massive scale at the moment,

and constant pressure is being applied toward ever-increasing abuse. You will have to live for a long time with such transgressions, and in all probability forever.

Crusading, however, is not the purpose of this volume. Defining the nature of our problems, restating the principles upon which our founding fathers pledged their sacred honor, applying those principles to our choices and solutions, and declaring our responsibilities and answering the question, "What can I do?" **is** the purpose of this book.

If we think through our responsibilities and act upon them we will have proven ourselves worthy of living as free men and women. If we do not, the consequences are inevitable.

The choice is still ours.

FOOTNOTES TO CHAPTERS

Chapter I
1   Benson, Ezra Taft, "The Proper Role Of Government," *The Freeman,* Foundation For Economic Education, November, 1976
2   Evans, M. Stanton, *The Liberal Establishment,* Devin-Adair Company, New York, 1965
3   Simon, William E., "Big Government And Our Economic Woes," *Readers Digest,* April, 1975 and Budget of U.S. Government 1981.
4   Evans, M. Stanton, *Clear And Present Danger,* p. 109, Harcourt, Brace, Jovanovick, Inc., 1975
5   Ibid, p. 110
6   Ibid, p. 106
7   Ibid, 1
8   *Human Events,* (Commission On Federal Paperwork 1976)
9   Lambro, Donald, *The Federal Rathole,* Arlington House, 1975
10   Wall Street Journal, June 17, 1976
11   National Taxpayers Union

Chapter II
1   "The Federal Budget In Brief, Fiscal Year 1974," p. 32/1975, p. 54, Executive Office of the President, Office of Management and the Budget.
2   Ibid and Budget of the U.S. Government 1981
3   Evans, M. Stanton, *Clear And Present Dangers,* p. 116, Harcourt, Brace, Jovanovich, Inc., 1975
4   Ibid and Budget of the U.S. Government 1981.
5   *U.S. News & World Report,* September 1, 1975
6   Lambro, Donald, *The Federal Rathole,* p. 173-200, Arlington House, 1975
7   Simon, William E., *The Wall Street Journal,* November 3, 1976
8   Evans, M. Stanton, *Human Events,* September 11, 1976
9   Ibid
10   Ibid

Chapter III
1   Russell, Dean, "Freedom Follow The Free Market," *Essays On Liberty,* Foundation For Economic Education, 1963
2   Ibid
3   Russell, Dean, "The Bill Of Rights," *Essays On Liberty,* Foundation For Economic Education, 1952
4   Young Presidents Club, Drake Hotel, Chicago, 1963
5   Crane, Hon. Philip M., *The Sum Of Good Government,* p. 153, Green Hill Publishers, Inc., 1976
6   Meltzer, Allan H., *Why Government Grows,* Green Hill Publishers, Inc., 1976
7   Ibid
8   Ibid
9   Crane, Hon., Phillip M., *The Democrat's Dilemma,* Henry Regnery Company, 1964
10   Jones, Jenken Lloyd, "Who Is Tampering America's Soul?" Star Free Press
11   Rafferty, Max, *Suffer, Little Children,* Devin-Adair Company, New York, 1962

Chapter IV

1   Friedman, Milton, "Economic Myths And Public Opinion," *The Alternative, An American Spectator,* January, 1974
2   Ibid
3   Rickenbacker, William, "Who's Afraid Of Hard Times," *Playboy Magazine,* 1974

Chapter V

1   Wilson, Hon., Robert (R-Calif.) *Battleline,* American Conservative Union
2   Tax Foundation, *Human Events,* November 27, 1976
3   Sennholz, Dr. Hans, Foundation For Economic Education Seminar, January 16, 1976
4   Stevenson, Adlai, Address at Colby College
5   Kennedy, John F., Statement on National television
6   Johnson, Lyndon B., Address to Congress, January 4, 1964
7   Evans, M. Stanton, *The Liberal Establishment,* Devin-Adair Company, New York, 1965

Chapter VI

1   Von Hayek, Frederich A., "Economic Myths Of Early Capitalism," Intercollegiate Studies Institute, Inc., 1960
2   "Too Big Or Not Too Big?" *Readers Digest,* p. 196, November, 1976
3   Evans, M. Stanton, *Clear And Present Dangers,* p. 124, Harcourt, Brace, Jovanovich, Inc., New York, 1975
4   Ibid
5   Friedman, Milton, *Capitalism And Freedom,* University Of Chicago Press, 1962
6   Crane, Hon., Phillip M., *The Sum Of Good Government,* p. 119 Green Hill Publishers, Inc.
7   Read, Leonard E., "The Exception Makers," *Essays On Liberty,* Vol. 5, 1958, Foundation For Economic Education

Chapter VII

1   Harvey, Paul, "Remember These Things," Chicago: Heritage Foundation, 1952
2   Author's note: I have often felt in light of today's conditions that if the term "pursuit of happiness" had been replaced with the work "property" the document would have gained both strength and ease in understanding. The term "pursuit of happiness" is drawn from the writings of John Locke and throughout he defines this as the endowed right to earn or inherit, and hold, private property.
3   Harvey, Paul, *The Rest Of The Story,* New York: Hanover House, 1956
4   McCullock Vs. Maryland, 1819

Chapter VIII

1   **Moreell, Ben, "The Communism - Via Majority Vote,"** *Essays On Liberty,* 1954, Foundation For Economic Education
2   Kappel, Frederick, *Vitality In A Business Enterprise,* New York: McGraw-Hill Book Company, 1960
3   Stone, Willis, "Fact Sheets" (Results of more than 17 years of research into budget reports, Congressional Records, Hoover Reports, etc.)
4   Ibid
5   Ibid
6   Ibid
7   Ibid
8   Ibid

Chapter IX
1 Bastiat, Frederick, *The Law,* Translation by Dean Russell, Foundation For Economic Education, 1963
2 Opitz, Rev. Edmund A. "Defining Freedom," *Essays On Liberty,* Foundation For Economic Education, 1963

Chapter X
1 "Constitution Of The Union Of Soviet Socialist Republics," Amended February 25, 1947, Foreign Languages Publishing House, Moscow

Chapter XI
1 Yutang, Lin., *The Gay Genius,* 1947

Chapter XII
1 Sutherland, Justice, George, *Constitutional Power And World Affairs,* 1919
2 Bastiat, Frederick, *The Law,* Translation by Dean Russell, Foundation For Economic Education, 1950

Chapter XIV
1 *Essays On Liberty,* Vol. 4, p. 239, Foundation For Economic Education
2 Ibid
3 *Essays On Liberty,* Vol. 10, p. 77, Foundation For Economic Education
4 Read, Leonard E., *Conscience Of The Majority,* Foundation For Economic Education, 1962
5 Ibid
6 Opitz, Reb. Edmund A., *The American System And Majority Rule,* Foundation For Economic Education

Chapter XVI
1 Roberts, Paul Craig, "The Political Economy Of Bureaucratic Imperialism," *Intercollegiate Studies Institute,* p. 3, Vol. 12, No. 1, Fall, 1976

Chapter XVII
1 Tocqueville, Alexis de, *Democracy In America,* Oxford University Press, New York, 1952
2 Friedman, Milton, *Capitalism And Freedom,* University Of Chicago Press, 1962
3 Ibid
4 Nock, Albert J., *Free Speech And Plain Language,* William Morrow & Company, 1937
5 Emerson, Ralph Waldo, "Self Reliance," *Essays,* Thomas Crowell Company, New York, 1926
6 Rogge, Benjamin A., "The Case For Economic Freedom," *The Freeman,* Foundation For Economic Education, September, 1963

BIBLIOGRAPHY

Aquinas, St. Thomas, *Truth*, Chicago: Henry Regnery Company, 1954

Aristotle, *Basic Works Of Aristotle*, ed. Richard Peter McKeon, New York: Random House, 1941

Bastiat, Frederic, *The Law*, translated by Dean Russell, Irvington-On-Hudson (N.Y.): Foundation For Economic Education, Inc., 1961

Bigongiari, Dina, *The Political Ideas of St. Thomas Aquinas*, New York: Hafner Publishing, Inc., 1953

Buckley, William F., Jr., *Up From Liberalism*, New York: Hillman Periodicals, Inc., 1959

Carson, Clarence B., *The Fateful Turn*, Irvington-On-Hudson (N.Y.): Foundation For Economic Education, 1963

Catlin, George, *The Story of Political Philosophers*, New York: McGraw Hill Book Company, 1939

Chamberlain, William Henry, *The Evolution Of A Conservative*, Chicago: Henry Regnery Company, 1959

Cobban, Alfred, *Edmund Burke And The Revolt Against The 18th Century*, New York: Macmillan Company, 1961

Coker, Francis William, *Readings In Political Philosophy*, New York: Macmillan Company, 1938

Crane, Philip M., *The Democrat's Dilemma*, Chicago: Henry Regnery Company, 1964

Crane, Philip M., *The Sum Of Good Government*, Ottawa, Illinois: Greenhill Publishing Company, 1976

Davenport, John, *The U.S. Economy*, Chicago: Henry Regnery Company, 1964

Dos Passos, John, *Occasions and Protests*, Chicago: Henry Regnery Company, 1964

Dunning, William A., *A History Of Political Theories*, New York: MacMillan Company, 1905

Emerson, Ralph Waldo, *Essays*, New York: Thomas Crowel Company, 1926

Essays On Liberty, Irvington-On-Hudson (N.Y.): Foundation For Economic Education, 1952 - 1976

The Essential Left, Marx, Engels, Lenin, New York: Barnes And Noble, 1961

Evans, M. Stanton, *The Fringe On Top*, New York: American Features, 1963

Evans, M. Stanton, *The Liberal Establishment*, New York: The Devin-Adair Company, 1965

Evans, M. Stanton, *The Revolt On Campus*, Chicago: Henry Regnery Company, 1961

Evans, M. Stanton, *Clear And Present Dangers*, New York: Harcourt, Brace, Jovanovich, 1976

The Federalist Paper, edited by Clinton Bossiter, New York: New American Library, 1961

Fertig, Lawrence, *Prosperity Through Freedom,* Chicago: Henry Regnery Company, 1961

Frederich, Carl J., *The Philosophy Of Hegel,* New York: Holt, Reinhart & Winston, 1961

Gibbon, Edward, *The Decline And Fall Of The Roman Empire,* 3 volumes, New York: Modern Library, 1937

Goldwater, Barry M., *The Conscience Of A Conservative,* Shepherdsville (Ky.): Victor Publishing Company, 1960

Harvey, Paul M., *Autumn Of Liberty,* New York: Hanover House, 1954

Harvey, Paul M., *Remember These Things,* Chicago: Heritage Foundation, 1952

Harvey, Paul M., *The Rest Of The Story,* New York: Hanover House, 1956

Von Hayek, Friedrich A., *The Road To Surfdom,* Chicago: University Of Chicago Press, 1944

Hazlitt, Henry, *Economics In One Lesson,* New York: Harper & Brothers, 1946

Harman, J. Judd, *Political Thought From Plato To The Present,* New York: McGraw-Hill Book Company, 1964

Hume, David, *An Enquiry Concerning Human Understanding,* Chicago: Henry Regnery Company, 1956

Hume, David, *Theory Of Politics,* ed. Frederick Watkins, Austin: University of Texas Press, 1953

Jones, Robert V., *The Challenge Of Liberty,* Chicago: Heritage Foundation, 1956

Kirk, Russell, *The Conservative Mind,* Chicago: Henry Regnery Company, 1953

Locke, John, *Essay Concerning Human Understanding,* Chicago: Henry Regnery Company, 1956

Locke, John, *A Letter Concerning Toleration,* New York: Macmillan Company, 1956

Locke, John, *Second Treatise Of Government,* New York: Macmillan Company, 1956

Machiavelli, Niccolo, *The Prince And The Discourses,* New York: Modern Library, 1950

MacKinnon, James, *Calvin And The Reformation,* New York: David McKay Company, 1936

Marx, Karl, *Capital,* New York: Modern Library, 1906

Marx, Karl, *The Communist Manifesto,* Chicago: Henry Regnery Company, 1961

Meyer, Alfred G., *Marxism: The Unity Of Theory And Practice,* Cambridge: Harvard University Press, 1954

McGovern, William M., *Strategic Intelligence And The Shape Of Tomorrow,* Chicago: Henry Regnery Company, 1961

Mill, John Stuart, *On Liberty*, Chicago: Henry Regnery Company, 1956

Montesquieu, Baron Charles de, *The Spirit Of Laws*, New York: Hafner Publishing Company, 1949

Plato, *The Republic*, translated by A. D. Lindsay, New York: E. P. Dutton & Company, 1957

Rafferty, Max, *Suffer, Little Children*, New York: The Devin-Adair Company, 1962

Read, Leonard E., *Elements Of Libertarian Leadership*, Irvington-On-Hudson (N.Y.): Foundation For Economic Education, Inc., 1965

Read, Leonard E., *The Free Market And Its Enemy*, Irvington-On-Hudson (N.Y.): Foundation For Economic Education, Inc., 1965

Read, Leonard E., *Why Not Try Freedom?*, Irvington-On-Hudson (N.Y.): Foundation For Economic Education, Inc., 1958

Richberg, Donald R., *Labor Union Monopoly*, Chicago: Henry Regnery Company, 1957

Roepke, Wilhelm, *Economics Of The Free Society*, Chicago: Henry Regnery Company, 1963

Rousseau, Jean Jacques, *The Social Contact And The Discourses*, New York: E. P. Dutton Company, 1913

Rudd, Augustin, *Bending Of The Twig*, Chicago: Heritage Foundation, 1957

Smith, Adam, *The Wealth Of Nations*, New York: Modern Library, 1928

Stanlis, Peter J., *Edmund Burke And The Natural Law*, Ann Arbor: University Of Michigan Press, 1958

Tocqueville, Alexis de, *Democracy In America*, New York: Oxford University Press, 1952

Voegelin, Eric, *Plato And Aristotle: Order And History*, Baton Rouge: Louisiana State University Press, 1957

Von Mises, Ludwig, *Human Action*, New Haven: Yale University Press, 1949

Von Mises, Ludwig, *Omnipotent Government: The Rise Of The Total State And Total War*, New Haven: Yale University Press, 1944

Weaver, Henry Grady, *The Mainspring Of Human Progress*, Irvington-On-Hudson (N.Y.): Foundation For Economic Education, Inc., 1953

Weaver, Richard M., *Ideas Have Consequences*, Chicago: University Of Chicago Press, 1948

Weaver, Richard M., *Visions Of Order*, Baton Rouge: Louisiana State University Press, 1964

Weyl, Nathaniel and Possony, Stefan, *The Geography Of Intellect*, Chicago: Henry Regnery Company, 1963

Wolin, Sheldon S., *Politics And Vision*, New York: Little, Brown & Company, 1960

Wormuth, Francis L., *The Origins Of Modern Constitutionalism,* New York: Harper & Row, 1949

McIlwain, Charles H., The Growth Of Political Thought In The West, New York: Macmillan Company, 1932

Mill, John Stuart, *Essential Works,* edited by Max Lerner, New York: Bantam Books, 1961

The following books are available from The Fisher Institute

QUANTITY   **TOTAL PRICE**

_____ copy of FUNDAMENTALS OF ECONOMICS: A
PROPERTY RIGHTS APPROACH by Dr. Svetozar
Pejovich. The inclusion of new property rights concepts up-
dates the field of economics in this basic textbook for beginning business/economics students and educated laymen.
258 pages. 51 charts and tables.

$11.95 (hardback)   _____

_____ copy of TAX LIMITATION, INFLATION & THE
ROLE OF GOVERNMENT by Milton Friedman. The
Nobel Laureate has been called the most influential economist of this era. This new book will give you a broad picture of economic research and a fascinating overview of free
market philosophy. It is sound public policy material. 110
pages, 15 graphs, 2 tables.

$5.95 (paperback)   _____

_____ copy of LIFE IN THE SOVIET UNION: A REPORT
CARD ON SOCIALISM by Dr. Svetozar Pejovich. A na-
tive of Yugoslavia, Dr. Pejovich uses new and revealing
economic facts about how Soviet citizens are *really* living —
a far cry from the Soviet government's propaganda. 101
pages, 11 charts & tables.

$4.95 (paperback); $9.95 (hardback)   _____

_____ copy of NATIONAL HEALTH CARE IN GREAT
BRITAIN: LESSONS FOR THE U.S.A. by Dr. John
Goodman, professor of economics, University of Dallas. This
is the first comprehensive study of the cradle-to-grave health
care system in Great Britain. Its economic realities should
provide lessons for U.S. proponents of similar programs. 210
pages, 15 charts & graphs.

$6.95 (paperback); $11.95 (hardback)   _____

_____ copy of THOSE GASOLINE LINES AND HOW THEY
GOT THERE by Dr. H. E. Merklein and William P. Mur-
chison, Jr. A Ph.D. economist/petroleum engineer and a
talented journalist combine to indict the massive government
bureaucracy for America's current energy shortage. Some
hard facts and incisive writing make this a book all American consumers can read and understand. 130 pages, 36
charts and graphs.

$5.95 (paperback); $10.95 (hardback)   _____

_____ copy of FISHER'S CONCISE HISTORY OF ECO-
NOMIC BUNGLING by Antony Fisher. Fisher uses 5,000
years of economic history, logic, wit, anecdote, and a keen
understanding to show how the free market system works
best to improve every citizen's economic well-being. 113
pages of fascinating reading.

$8.95 (hardback); $2.95 (paperback)   _____

Prepaid orders shipped postage free. If you wish to be billed, a minimum of $1.00 will be added for
postage & handling...$ _____
(Plus 50¢ per book state tax if buyer resides in Texas)

Enclosed is my payment in full of.. $ _____

Name _____

Title _____ Company _____

Address _____

City _____ State _____ Zip _____

Please send information about the Fisher Institute ☐